Toward a Whole
Language Classroom

Toward a Whole Language Classroom: Articles from *Language Arts*, 1986–89

Selected by
Barbara Kiefer

National Council of Teachers of English
1111 Kenyon Road, Urbana, Illinois 61801

Production Editor: David A. Hamburg

Cover Design: Michael J. Getz; cover illustration by Nicholas J. Getz

Interior Design: Tom Kovacs for TGK Design

NCTE Stock Number 54964-3020

It is the policy of NCTE in its journals and other publications to provide a
forum for the open discussion of ideas concerning the content and the teaching of English and the language arts. Publicity accorded to any particular point
of view does not imply endorsement by the Executive Committee, the Board
of Directors, or the membership at large, except in announcements of policy,
where such endorsement is clearly specified.

Library of Congress Cataloging-in-Publication Data

Toward a whole language classroom : articles from Language arts, 1986–89 /
    selected by Barbara Kiefer.
        p.   cm.
    ISBN 0-8141-5496-4
    1. Language experience approach in education—United States. I. Kiefer,
Barbara Zulandt, 1944-   . II. National Council of Teachers of English.
III. Language arts.
LB1576.T68   1991
372.6—dc20   90-48614
                                                                       CIP

Contents

Preface

As this book goes to press, interest in the whole language approach is burgeoning. Thousands of teachers are looking for ways to incorporate student-centered, collaborative teaching strategies into their classrooms. This collection of articles draws heavily upon the experiences of reflective teacher-researchers who have adapted approaches based on the whole language philosophy to meet the unique learning styles of their students. The articles were drawn from issues of *Language Arts,* the membership journal of the Elementary Section of the National Council of Teachers of English, and were originally published between 1986 and 1989. It is hoped that they will help readers make the transition to classroom practices based on the spirit of the whole language philosophy.

1 *Writing*

What Am I Supposed to Do While They're Writing?

Mary K. Simpson

Emphasis, in the teaching of writing, has shifted from a narrow focus on end product to a broader view, encompassing the entire recursive process of producing a composition, from prewriting to publication. Teachers who have incorporated process writing into their classroom structure no longer assign writing and then move off to a safe distance and wait, red pen in hand, to evaluate student effort. Instead, we form a partnership with our students. We serve as instructors, listeners, and commenters. We offer suggestions, encouragement, and expertise. We structure a learning environment that encourages experimentation, provides support for beginning authors, and challenges students to revise until their writing is an accomplishment of which they can be proud. Language arts teachers strive to be caring, sensitive, demanding listeners, who see potential in a piece and in an author, where a casual observer might see only failure. We recognize our students' varying abilities to use language as a tool in communication and applaud their tentative efforts to find a voice. We provide the human connection between writer and critic so that the piece never becomes more important than the struggling author.

As I made my personal transition from an isolated-skills instructor and composition assigner/evaluator to a fellow participant in the writing-workshop environment in my classroom, one of my major concerns was to redefine *my* role in the classroom, as my students were involved in the writing process. Would I sit back and observe them soaring gracefully through revision, as if they were born to be part of a writing community? Would I wander from group to group catching snatches of discussion, encouraging when necessary, as my fledgling revisers practiced the techniques of supporting young authors who were attempting to communicate to readers? Or would I be an aggressive, active participant modeling flight for my novices?

Over time, my role was defined by the students, as they communicated their needs to me. In an atmosphere of acceptance, sharing, and honesty, the students made their expectations of me very clear. Taking into account their expectations, my instructional goals, and my own personality, I identified nine tasks that I had assigned to myself over the course of the year. Then I asked myself, "How did I translate those nine roles into actual classroom practice?" As a result of examining my behavior in the classroom, listening to tapes, observing videos, and writing daily impressions, I recognized things I had done and said that contributed to my performance in each role. Performing these tasks was my contribution to supporting my students during the writing process.

First, I served as a student's most ardent admirer and most astute critic, sometimes functioning in both roles simultaneously. I made it my business to see potential in a person and a piece of writing where others might see none, and I provided feedback that guaranteed the opportunity for progress. Specifically, I complimented improvement and pointed out what the author had done well. "You are very successful when you write about people in your life." There were times when I let the author know that the basic idea was good, even though changes were required. I helped the author to recognize a clever idea, but lack of development. I complimented the use of a successful technique, such as preparing a reader for a character's method of escape in an adventure story. I suggested that the piece was ripe for a sequel. I encouraged the author to think when he responded "I don't know" to a question. As an author, he must know his story and characters. Sometimes, I refused to accept the author's first suggestions for change. Instead, I encouraged him to think through two or three options. There were times when I encouraged a student to expand a piece with sensitive questioning because it was often clear that he knew more than he was telling. Often, I suggested that the addition of specific details would enhance believability. I found that interchanging the roles of admirer and critic was a very demanding task. It required a genuine sensitivity to the needs of the student.

Second, I taught the writer to internalize the reader role, so that she communicated her intended meaning to others. I helped her learn from an experience in which audience understanding was very different from what she intended, where she was surprised by her listeners' "wrong" interpretation. I tried to help her understand the effect of her words on a reader. We often discussed writer and reader roles, that a writer had to be a creator/critic of her own work, so that she could anticipate readers' questions. We discussed point of view and its effect on the reader's interpretation. Mature writers often find it difficult to operate as creators and critics of their own work, so students need to develop an understanding of how these two aspects of communication, writing and reading, must be used recursively by an author, so that she becomes her own best critic.

Third, I aided students in their search for voice. Writing is a process of self-discovery, where students gradually recognize that they have authoritative information to share and that they can communicate this information by writing in a tone that the reader will recognize as genuine. Students perceive themselves as knowledgeable as they allow themselves to be drawn out by a tactful, but demanding questioner. I helped the author to clarify his own thinking. Often that meant letting him "talk out" what he meant by expanding verbally. I had to make myself wait for the author to respond. He sometimes complained that he had no ideas for improving his own piece, and, as a teacher, I had to exercise judgment, deciding if the student was asking to be spoon-fed. I drew the author out, so that I could reinforce new or better ideas. "What are you thinking?" I asked him. Often, I requested more specific details. I reinforced the success that resulted when an author wrote from his own experience. Writing about incidences and characters *beyond* his experience could result in superficiality and lack of development. Sometimes, I had to limit other students' suggestions for solutions. Really important points had to be addressed by the author. As the students gained self-confidence and a belief in their ability to communicate, their writing voices got stronger and stronger. They wrote from their hearts about things that mattered to them.

Fourth, I protected an author as she offered her discovered meaning to an audience for comments. Students do not necessarily have the ability to screen suggestions and comments as to their appropriateness and applicability to a particular piece of writing. This skill requires a maturity and strength of self-concept that may be beyond the reach of many children. It is, therefore, possible that, without the support of a sensitive teacher, they may be too open in their acceptance of criticism. Constantly, I "read" the author carefully, watching for signs of frustration, if there were too many suggested changes. I attended to her reactions to comments. Did she become red-eyed? Did her body language communicate discomfort? I helped the author understand that a piece that is very rich in possibilities may elicit many comments. An author needs to interpret students' suggestions as a compliment to her ability to create. At times, I had to bail the author out if the elaborations suggested by others were too involved. I helped her establish her own boundaries for the piece. I helped the author decide which of the points mentioned in the revision groups were the most important. Many comments were distracting to her focus, related to unimportant details. I reminded the author that she had a choice of whether to take advice. Perhaps, most important, I allowed the author to maintain ownership of her piece, by asking her: "What would you improve?", "What problems do you see?", "What changes are needed?", "What do you think you want to do?", or "Do you feel comfortable with any of this?" On a regular basis, I needed to remind myself that my authors were children and sometimes needed a supportive adult to help them define their relationship to the group.

Fifth, I modeled appropriate group responses, questions, and techniques, while simultaneously individualizing instruction for the author, using the format of a conference-in-a-group setting, when we shared writing in revision groups. I encouraged others to wait while the author made the first comment about his writing. I encouraged a search for the strongest idea. Time was allowed to pass in both thought and discussion. Students need closure, and they would often grasp at *any* answer. I directed oral brainstorming or exploration of possibilities, in support of an author who was "stuck." I set standards for responses to the writing, always being honest in my praise. I guided students in the discussion of the main issues. They often suggested minor changes, rather than directing attention to the author's major task of communicating meaning. I encouraged the revisers to be specific in their comments. "What *exactly* do you want to know?" And, always at the end of the discussion of a piece of writing, I thanked the author. Again, doing two tasks at once was difficult. Individualization and small-group instruction occurred simultaneously.

Sixth, I placed the draft in a process context and the author in a student context. In the words of Donald M. Murray (1985), "The student needs to know where the draft is in the writing process so the student can apply the skills appropriate to that stage of the process" (p. 168). For example, an author might be discovering focus, a stage where she would ignore punctuation. Murray continues, "The student also needs to realize that he or she is developing as a writer. A writing history is being written through the drafts, and the teacher should remind the student of this individual history" (p. 169). A teacher might say, "You're making us care about your characters! I can remember when. . . ." I tried to instill confidence by asking the author, "What are your plans for tomorrow?" I referred to the author's reading of a previous study and the resulting comments. Had she utilized that experience to improve the piece under discussion? I responded positively when an author successfully tried a previously unsuccessful genre. The key was to focus on *any* improvement to model future efforts. I pointed out that her change/rewrite was worth the effort. Students needed help in focusing their attention on the task that is appropriate at a particular moment in the process of writing. Furthermore, students needed to be reminded of where they had been in terms of their writing, so they could map their own writing destinations.

Seventh, I integrated skill instruction within the context of revising a piece of writing that the student cared about. Skills are meaningful when they help an author transmit his meaning to a reader. I called attention to the skill that an author needed to focus on in his second draft by identifying individual weaknesses and providing instruction. When needed, I taught the mechanical techniques of revision in a meaningful context: notetaking, using arrows to insert/relocate, and making changes in the margin. In addition, I taught the skills of making internal changes in a draft: finding a place to insert change, encouraging the generation of alternatives to traditional endings, suggesting the use of descriptive details to aid believability, and pointing to an excellent choice of words/phrase or suggesting change. Especially, I emphasized the skills of character development: using examples in character description (show rather than tell), changing narration to dialogue to allow the characters to speak for themselves, connecting action of characters to their personalities, recognizing characters must be motivated to change, and accounting for all characters at the end. I found that students learned skills more readily and integrated them in future writing when instruction was directly relevant to their own writing needs.

Eighth, I monitored individual progress, as an author functioned in a revision group. I watched to see if the author maintained her identity within the group, approached the group with self-confidence, and established ownership of her piece; if she used the advice/suggestions of the group wisely to improve her writing and learned from experience; and if she developed the skills of group interaction and helped and supported a fellow author. In the fluid atmosphere of the writing workshop, I was often concerned that I would become so swept up in the enthusiasm of the groups that I would forget to focus my attention on individuals, diagnosing and encouraging when necessary. It was important to me never to lose sight of individual progress.

Finally, my most important contribution was to maintain the human connection. For many authors, their writing and their selves are inseparable. The teacher must remember that, of the two, the author is the most important. It is a courageous act to write from your heart, share that writing with your peers, and accept their critique. Blossoming authors have a fragility that must be respected and protected.

At first, I thought the hard part was the identification of these tasks. Was I wrong! What was really difficult was measuring up to my own standards. Having developed this list of objectives for myself as a writing teacher, I had something against which to measure my own performance. Curriculum guides and instructor manuals include lists of skills for the students to achieve, but, often, they do not enumerate the tasks that the teacher should master. So, in my innocence, I composed a mastery list of my own. There were days when I wished I hadn't. Days when I fell short of my self-expectations. But frequent self-evaluation, although painful at times, did keep me moving in the direction I wanted to go. And, on the days when I had done my job well, I could accept some of the credit for smiles on the writers' faces, and I knew that I was making a contribution to our classroom writing community.

Reference

Murray, D. M. *A Writer Teaches Writing.* Boston: Houghton Mifflin, 1985.

[Language Arts *63, no. 7 (1986): 680–84*]

2 *Writing*

The Writer's Inside Story

Carin Hauser

Our writers' workshop starts with a flurry of activity. Appointed students pass out folders. Writers review the contents to find their starting places for the day's work, rereading, rethinking the pieces they wrote the day before. On the board, one student entitles a list "CONFRENCES NEEDED" and five children hurry to sign up. Several pairs of writers are nestled in the corners of the classroom, reading drafts to each other for feedback. Some third-grade students, like Lindsay, draft new stories, pencils bobbing across the pages, undisturbed by the industry around them.

For several days, Lindsay had planned to write a story about the birth of her sister. She writes the piece quickly, pausing several times to reread what she had already put down on paper. This article describes Lindsay's development as a writer while she participated in our classroom workshops and, in particular, of her development as a reviser of her writing.

My research into Lindsay's writing evolved from several questions, questions at the heart of the design for our writing program: What does revision mean to a third-grade writer? Why do young students revise? What is the role of "writers' talk" in nurturing successful young authors?

For several years, I had watched my classes of gifted third graders grow into a community of writers who supported and challenged each other in their endeavors of authorship. We wrote a lot (including me). We also talked a lot about our writing—what worked, what caused problems, how we solved problems, what particulars sounded good in a story, how stories fit together in surprising ways, what qualities made writing good. We developed a grammar unique to writers who get stuck and struggle, as well as experience success.

My intuition told me that writing conferences help nurture these children in becoming confident and effective writers. I hoped my research would help me to define further the relationship between a child's revision strategies and the writers' talk that was an important part of our workshops. Writers' talk includes the one-to-one conferring between writers (teacher-student and student-student) as well as class discussions of writing, either that of the students or professionally published authors. In order to explore my questions about revision, I focused on Lindsay's development, while noting the changes and interactions of the other students.

"The New Baby": Moving toward Clarity and Voice

Lindsay liked her story about her new baby sister; she chose it over others in her folder for publishing. I have typed the piece as she wrote it on her first draft. The hand-printed text in the margins and within the text shows how Lindsay later revised her story, as do the cross-outs.

]T̸H̸E N̸E̸W B̸A̸B̸Y [

because she has people said blue pretty and eyes suits cute

In 1980 in the winter my mom had my sister she got lots of presents. And I was real jealous. I was just 4 when she was born. When it was time to pickup Megan and Mom it was snowing. I think it was blizzard. ~~Oh! well let's not get into a conversation. Let's get on with the story.~~

¶When we came to pick up Megan and Mom up we went into the hospital and Mom was sitting there with Megan sitting on her lap. Then the nurse told me I had pretty blue eyes. Then she let me hold Megan.

I wasn't jealous much anymore

¶She was cute and furry. That's only because she had a furry suit on.

¶ Now Megan's 4. She still likes me to hold her.

During our publishing conference, Lindsay read her story to me, and as she read, she made editing changes, adding some of the forgotten punctuation and capitalization. The conference setting required her to be a critical editor of her own work; her relationship to her story changed, requiring a different kind of reading.

Later during the conference, I asked Lindsay to tell me the main idea of the story. She replied, without hesitation, "How I felt when Megan was born." I asked her to look carefully at her story to make sure that everything in it helped to express her main idea. I also suggested putting an arrow in the margin wherever she felt she should give additional information. I didn't tell her where that information was necessary; that decision was hers. My questions were intended to provoke her to think more deeply about the incident, to encourage her to expand her piece: Why was Lindsay jealous? How did she feel when the nurse told her she had pretty eyes and let her hold the new baby?

When Lindsay went back to her seat, she made several changes on her draft in response to my interventions. She later published her story on special book paper and shared it with the class. Lindsay also showed her classmates her draft and the revisions she had made. These revisions both clarified the meaning of the story and gave the piece a stronger voice. She accomplished this by adding details to already existing sentences and paragraphs and by crossing out sentences which didn't move her story forward. When Lindsay stated her main idea, she seemed to discover a controlling focus for her story—her verbalization of this focus during the conference helped her to make decisions to omit some of the sentences on her draft.

When Lindsay analyzed her revisions of "The New Baby," she noted that she had added the two sentences at the end because "I didn't want them to think she's a baby still." I asked her whom she meant by "them." She replied, "Whoever reads the story." Lindsay realizes that her audience does not have all the information she has, and through revision, she tries to help her reader. She also revised in order to "let the reader know more about me."

A Writer's Emergency

Early one fall morning, I found a note from Lindsay in my emergency folder. She had been working on a story about her friend's birthday party. The note stated:

> My problem is I don't know if I should put the part about the presents in the story. I don't know if I should put it in a different story.

In her draft of the birthday story, Lindsay had devoted only one line to telling about the birthday presents. Even though she called this issue a problem, she retained a sense of options; she named two options in her note. However, with one of the options came the frustration of confronting an already-written story and making major changes, changes that would alter the *structure* of the story.

Up until this point, Lindsay's writing told a story that progressed linearly in time; she told what happened at the beginning of the event and continued until she felt she had narrated the entire incident. Lindsay's concern about this writing showed; she discussed her "problem" with me as we walked to the cafeteria. In trying to help her, I asked Lindsay if the opening of presents was an important or exciting part of the party. "Oh, yes!" was her reply. I suggested that she try starting the story with the most exciting part.

During the next day's workshop, Lindsay wrote a new lead for her story on a separate sheet of paper. On the first draft, she crossed out the first four sentences. I have typed her story as she wrote it the first time; the new lead appears under the first draft.

Amanda's Party

On Columbus day which was Monday Oct. 8th Amanda had a party at showbiz pizza place. First we had to go to Amanda's house. When everybody had arrived we started opening presents. Then we got into the cars. On the way Amanda was complaining about her lose tooth. She said, "I won't be able to eat pizza!" So I said, "Just pull it out!" Then she went to wiggle it and it came out. Blood was coming out real fast so she bit on a tissue. And she said, "I losht my shoe!" I said, "You didn't lose a SHOE!" When we finally got to showbiz it was pretty dark. Then we got our tokens and played skeeball. I got 21 tokens but Amanda only had 19 so I gave her 1. Then we went to skeeball. I played all my tokens on skeeball except 3 and those were for the place you dive into some neat red balls. Then you climb up a net and up to a big yellow slide. Then after pizza and cake we had to go home. Amanda went in a different car then me. I was real upset. I wanted to sit with her. But anyway I'd see her in the morning.

The End

Lindsay's new lead:

"When are we going to open the presents?" yelled Amanda while everybody was rushing through the door. When everybody came we started to open presents. She got a cabbage patch miniture. A book that told things to do with kids in Washington, D.C. She got a lot of other things too.

In revising this story, Lindsay exerted a new kind of control over her writing—she had changed the structure of the piece. She crossed out an entire section of her story and rewrote it. The piece still moved through time linearly, but Lindsay directed the pace of the movement; she was in charge of the unfolding of her story. An internal adviser seemed to be at work as Lindsay revised this story. This adviser helped her decide what to put in her story and what to leave out. Lindsay was learning that there are options to consider in writing. She didn't have to write everything she remembered about the incident. With the help of the internal adviser, she could assign different "weights of importance" to the parts of her experience, deciding which parts to include and which to omit.

Lindsay shared her birthday story drafts with the whole class the next day. She showed the other students how she had changed the first part of her story, explaining that it now had a better lead. She called this kind of lead a "middle of the action" lead. This term has become part of the writers' talk of the class.

In writing this piece, Lindsay discovered and defined in her own terms a writing issue. She discussed this issue with the other writers in the class. Other students started experimenting with middle-of-the-action leads. This exchange of writers' talk helps all of the students develop an awareness of how "real" writers work. The modeling of real writing problems and their solutions unleashes a powerful teaching potential among students.

Becoming a Critical Reader

Lindsay's struggles with her drafts, especially the longer ones, showed that she was tackling more complex issues of writing. She was particularly concerned that her organization help her readers understand and enjoy her writing.

Lindsay defined the hardest part of working with one of her longest pieces, "The Ballet Show," as making the decision on how to organize her information. "The Ballet Show" piece consisted of four sections, which she reworked deliberately one by one. She made her decisions on organization in this way:

> I read it one by one (section by section), and then I decided how other people would like it—separate (stories) or together. So I thought it would be a little more exciting (as a chapter book).

Lindsay considered her audience in making her decision. She had added another dimension to the multifaceted internal adviser, that of a critical reader. As a critical reader of her own work, she holds the needs of her audience as a gauge against which she makes decisions about revision. The rereading requires Lindsay to question her choices of words, sentences, organization (as in "The Ballet Show"), topic, and even punctuation.

Using the Conference

As Lindsay became more confident as a writer, her attitude toward the conference changed. Early in the school year, she seemed more content to wait for my lead, or my prompt as we discussed her work. Because she participated in many successful conferences, Lindsay gradually became able to direct the conference, to use it for her writing needs.

In early January, Lindsay and I conferred about "A Day in D.C." As she read her story to me, she added the punctuation and capitalization that she had forgotten on her draft. When I retold Lindsay's story, she took charge of the conference. Interrupting me during my retelling, she offered more information about the aquarium, one of the sites she visited during the trip. In the margin, she put an arrow to remind herself that she wanted to add that information, to "fatten it up." When I retold a confusing part of the story, Lindsay announced that it wasn't clear, and she described how she would change it. Lindsay made the decisions about what she would add or change. She directed the conference based on what she perceived as the needs of the writing.

In the conference setting, Lindsay reads her piece as a detached consumer of her writing. The conference seems to make strong demands of the internal adviser. This adviser analyzes the writing to make sure the intended meaning is clear. Lindsay makes notes independently in the margins of her draft to remind herself of what she wants to change. She also becomes a very critical editor, finding the spots which need punctuation and capitalization. What is my role? Listener, summarizer, and consultant.

The workshop helps each writer develop an active internal adviser. By analyzing and responding to each others' stories, the students internalize useful strategies of questioning the writing to ensure clarity, as Lindsay does. Talking about the process of making the drafts, the revisions, and the decision making, helps the children to define, explore, and create options in their writing.

Understanding Revision: An Evolving Process

Lindsay's understanding of revision evolved through her positive experiences with writing (including publishing) and through the rich interaction among her classmates during the workshops. The conferring process enabled and encouraged her growth as a reviser, too. She finds revision to be an integral part of her writing—she revises throughout the process. In response to my question about whether she revises on her first drafts, she emphatically replied, "Of course!" She brought me a draft of her Cabbage Patch Premie story to explain the reasons for the revisions she had made:

> Well, you know all the info. They—the reader or readers—don't
> know what's in your mind . . . in my Cabbage Patch Premie story,

the boys need to know more info. You make it for the reader to read. They may not understand how it is to have a Cabbage Patch Premie.

Lindsay shared these insights with me during an interview in early April. She responded seriously to my questions about why she revises her stories. As I made notes, she watched me intently, clarifying her statements, making sure that I understood why she felt revision was, for her, the most difficult part of writing. Lindsay explained:

When I write a sentence, sometimes I stop dead in the sentence and I think about the last sentence I wrote. If it's not clear and I say to myself if the sentence behind that isn't clear for the reader, I should fatten it up. The whole purpose of writing the story is for the reader to read it and understand it and enjoy it.

She has internalized the need to revise as she composes, questioning herself to make sure the reader will understand her story. This is a reflective act, requiring a rereading and a rethinking of the words she puts down on paper. This reflection requires Lindsay to examine the writing as a would-be reader, putting the internal adviser to work.

Implications

1. Talking about the "inside story" of writing, or about the revisions writers make on their drafts, helps all children understand the integral role that revising plays in the writing process. The writers' workshop, or the writing program, should focus on different kinds of writers' talk:
   —talk that leads to a clarification of meaning in the story
   —talk that examines the reasons for the revisions made in the story
2. A great deal of "writers' talk," both in one-to-one conferences and in class discussions externalizes the options that authors face as they work. When experiences with writing are positive, varied, and rich in interaction, children internalize the sense of options, becoming special readers of their own writing. The external process, centering on modeling and talking, encourages the internal process.
3. The conference encourages children to examine their writing from a critical viewpoint. The child's reading of the story out loud especially helps the writer begin to edit the piece. Retelling also shows the child that the writing has value.

4. Retelling the story helps the author analyze the writing for clarity.

5. Not all children will follow Lindsay's pattern of development as a writer. However, all writers grow if they can see how the revision process of other writers works. Both student and teacher modeling help writers grow.

Although my research centered on Lindsay's composing strategies, what she taught me went far beyond the implication of our writers' workshop. The depth of her insights into her own learning amazes me. All I had to do to tap these insights was listen, pen and journal in hand. Her earnest enthusiasm in helping me "get it right" and understand her process of revision reaffirmed for me that teaching's richest moments are actually moments of learning. Our classroom community of writers nurtures more than writers—we support learners and teachers, too.

[Language Arts *63, no. 2 (1986): 153–59*]

3 *Writing/Thinking*

First Grade Thinkers
Becoming Literate

Carol S. Avery

On January 29, 1985, the morning after the Challenger tragedy, Stephen, age six, came into the classroom and stated, "I know how the space shuttle blew up." Somewhat incredulously, I responded, "You do? Tell me."

Stephen proceeded to tell me with certainty that something went wrong with the rockets—the fuel, he thought. "The fuel blew up, the rockets blew up and then the whole space shuttle blew up. I heard it on TV."

The more I dialogued with Stephen, the more solidified he became in his position that the fuel caused the disaster. As Stephen spoke, his classmates nearby became interested, and soon a score of first graders had answers to questions the entire world was only beginning to ask that morning.

As the children's teacher, I was distressed at the quickness with which they found and accepted *final* solutions. I had been trying to instill another way of thinking. In daily writing and reading workshops the children were always in search of meaning from the written word. As they shared and responded to texts authored by peers and professionals, I encouraged them to withhold judgment and consider a diversity of interpretations and ideas. In the context of the reading and writing curricula, these children were becoming careful listeners, perceptive questioners, and strong thinkers. Now, I wondered, were they becoming literate?

The children had responded to world events in a manner unlike the norm of inquiry in the classroom. My students were competent readers and writers; but being literate, I believe, is more than being *able* to read and write, and more than *being* a reader and a writer. Mastering the skills of reading and writing and applying those skills only in classroom settings is not the attainment of literacy. Donald Graves has stated, "To be literate is to listen, to observe intently, see what the moment gives and ask 'What does it mean?' "

My interactions with the children that morning impelled me to expand the processes of our reading and writing workshops to all areas of our curriculum. The little writing we had done as a part of math, science, and social studies had been confined to writing math problems and summary learnings at the end of units of study. I needed to demonstrate to my students ways to use writing as a tool to make sense of, and to form meaning from, the world around them, to raise new questions and seek new answers as circumstances changed. In this way, I hoped, they could experience the empowerment that true literacy brings.

The same elements that formed the structure of our writing workshop would be transferred to this experience. It was important that students have time to write and explore their ideas. They also would need to share their writing, receive responses from and engage in dialogue with others, and have opportunities to rewrite and revise their thinking and writing. Most important, students would need to have a large part in forming questions, exploring ideas, and drawing conclusions so that they might more fully take responsibility for their learning.

What follows is the story of this first grade class from February through June. While the examples are of six- and seven-year-olds, I believe the process and components can be the same for any grade level.

Writing for Learning and Thinking across the Curriculum

I first introduced the writing procedures into the science curriculum with a unit on astronomy. Our class was scheduled to visit the high school planetarium four times during February. Immediately upon returning from our first visit, I asked the children to write what they remembered or what was important to them.

Writing *before* discussion is important. Toby Fulwiler (1985) says doing so gives writers opportunity to discover their thoughts before they speak (a particularly enabling factor for reticent children); commits writers to a stand; and allows writers to arrive at their own thoughts without first being directed by others—including the teacher. Therefore, Fulwiler believes, "more personal writing is a direct route to more autonomous thinking."

After committing their thoughts about the planetarium visit to paper, the children shared this writing with a partner, and then a few children shared with the entire group. Some children wrote about the bus ride. One or two wrote pieces that began with our departure, included one sentence about the planetarium, and ended with our return. The majority of the writing was of one or two short statements, such as: "We learned that the sun is a star," "There are nine planets," "Comets are sorta like stars but they're not stars."

Our group sharing and discussions helped form questions which we wrote on charts and read before our next visit: What is the difference between a comet and a star? Why are some planets hot and some cold? If the sun is a star, why can't we see it at night? The questions helped focus the children's thinking during the next planetarium visits. After each visit and also after reading books or viewing filmstrips, we followed the steps of writing, sharing, discussing, and writing again. Children wrote their new learnings and ideas which they kept in folders and which we called logs. (A new log was started with each unit of study and eventually each child had three or four logs of writing.)

After the last planetarium visit, I asked the children to read through their planetarium logs and then to write a new piece about some aspect of this unit which interested them. These writings were not just facts strung together; most of them revealed the children's search for answers to questions they had raised.[1] Jared wrote:

> There are nine planets. Mercury is the planet closest to the sun. Mercury is hot. Earth is not hot because earth is not close to the sun. Venus is another planet. Mars is another planet too. You could not live on some planets because they are too cold or too hot. Only earth.

Billy wrote:

> When comets get near the sun it makes a tail. The tail turns away from the sun. Comets are as big as Manheim Township. Comet's orbits looks like a cigar!!!! Comets go very fast! I like comets.

The astronomy unit established an expected procedure of using writing beyond the confines of the writing workshop. When we began our dinosaur unit, the children wrote in their logs after viewing filmstrips and after listening to books about dinosaurs. For variety, the sharing time that followed was sometimes done in pairs, sometimes in small groups, or occasionally in the whole group. Children wrote additional ideas for their logs sometimes during, sometimes after the sharing. Throughout the sharing and learning process, I moved among them asking: "How do you know this?" "Why is this important?" "What do *you* think about this?" So many ideas emerged! The learning

---

[1] Children used invented spelling in their writing. Standard spelling as well as punctuation is used for clarity in all children's writing throughout this manuscript.

community became a resource for each individual as they asked each other questions and pooled their knowledge and hypotheses.

The class became interested in two particular questions in regard to dinosaurs: Why did the dinosaurs die? What color were dinosaurs? The children suggested many theories during the writing and discussion process. They were not content with absolute answers. In fact, they were excited to discover *many* possibilities.

At the end of the unit, I told the children to read through their dinosaur logs and write an organized piece on dinosaurs. As they put the logs away, I urged them to remember all they knew about good writing—strong leads, interesting information, focused ideas, clarity, making sense to other readers. They plunged into these pieces. "This is fun!" "Listen to my lead." "Can we do this tomorrow?" I believe their enthusiasm resulted from feeling involved with and in control of their learning. All the talking and writing had expanded the children's knowledge and understandings; they were eager to share their ideas with other audiences. Courtney's piece began:

> Roar! Roar! Roar! This is the sound of the ancient dinosaurs. They roamed the earth many years ago. They were terrible. We still don't know what color they were . . . They just guess green. But soon the dinosaurs started to die. No one knows for sure how they died. Some scientists say it got too cold. Some scientists say the land coughed and volcanos blew up. Some . . .

Amanda wrote:

> Boom! A star fell to the ground. The dinosaurs died. Dinosaurs lived millions of years ago. Dinosaurs could be pink or red or yellow or green or white or blue or orange or even polka dotted. . . .

Writing became the expected, even anticipated, mode of learning throughout the school day. In math, children not only wrote story problems, but also explanations of math processes. Janelle wrote about addition:

> Addition is adding means + the plus sign means you join 2 numbers and you get a big number like 8 + 3 = 11 and here's another one 2 + 8 = 10. Melissa had 9 cookies and her mother made two more cookies and now Melissa has 11 cookies.

Before instruction on the addition of double-digit numbers, I asked them to try solving the problem 31 + 42 and then to explain how they did it or to simply state they didn't know how and why. Patrick wrote:

> I added 3 and 4 That was 7 and then I added 2 and 1 that was 3—
> so it was 73.

Billy wrote:

> I don't know what this is because there are too much numbers.

A few days later, after instruction, children completed the same problem, wrote about their learning process, and then looked at their first explanations to see their own concept growth.

In March, I brought forsythia branches into the classroom to force blooming. I did not tell the children this was forsythia, but rather, asked them to observe and try to discover for themselves what this was. Each day the children recorded in logs the changes they saw. Their daily writing reflected the revision in their thinking as the blossoms appeared. Chad wrote:

> It looks like something that blooms and dies again. It has branches. It has leaves. It looks like any other plant and its branches are skinny and it looks like a plant from a flower shop.

And the next day:

> Since yesterday it has changed a lot. It use to have leaves on it. But now it has one flower on it My guess about is its a flower bush!

And after the weekend:

> On Friday it had only little bit of flowers. Since Saturday and Sunday it has bloomed. Now it has hundreds of flowers on it. It looks like a flower bush that were picked out of a flower garden. I think they are buttercups.

Troy wrote:

> I think it is a pussywillow that hasn't bloomed yet—that is a late bloomer. [Troy had just learned to read Robert Kraus's book *Leo the Late Bloomer.*]

And five days later:

> It bloomed a lot of flowers. It could have been a pussy willow that bloomed through.

On the sixth day Courtney slipped a note on my desk that said:

> Forsythia My grandmother told me I asked her what was a plant that had yellow flowers.

When Courtney explained to the class how she knew, she said: "Well, I asked my Grandma. I told her what it looked like and she said forsythia. But I wanted to be sure, so then I asked a couple more people. I asked my Mom and my Aunt Debbie and they both said forsythia so I figured it probably was." Courtney's observations and questioning led her not only to seek an answer, but to validate her answer with more than one source.

In late spring, after the class had finished listening to Roald Dahl's classic *James and the Giant Peach*, we went to the library to learn more about the six oversized creatures from Dahl's book: ladybug, spider, earthworm, centipede, grasshopper, and glow worm. The librarian pointed out poetry books, nonfiction books, junior encyclopedias, and study prints as possible sources. We instructed the children to look and read until they were "filled up," then to close their books and to write what seemed important.

What followed was a lot of noise and bustle—the result of first graders reading, writing, talking, thinking, discovering. Overheard were:

- Jon telling one classmate after another, "The ladybug was named after Mary, Jesus' mother."

- Jeff saying, "I wrote something I think is important. You see this is about the earthworm and how it eats *soil*."

- Colleen: "I just learned that spiders have *nine eyes!*"

- Another Jeff: "Centipedes can be poisonous. Did you know that?" He read the encyclopedia to me to prove his point.

We took many of these books to the classroom and established a shelf for each creature. Among the materials we kept there were writing folders where children placed their contributions. The children frequently gathered in pairs or small groups to read through the folders and discuss the ideas. Some children brought books from home to add to the shelves.

The children's thinking processes were evident in their writing. Katie wrote a page on spiders (an interest of hers from our reading of *Charlotte's Web*) that began:

> Spiders hang from their silk when they want to see a closer view.

Katie wondered *why* a spider would drop down on a strand of silk and put her own idea (hypothesis) into her writing. She also recalled Charlotte doing just this at the fair. Katie synthesized new information into what she already knew to formulate her hypothesis. She continued:

> Some spiders are poisonous like this. It is black and little of red on its body.

She described a poisonous spider from a picture in a book. Then she wrote:

> Spiders have two parts. Spiders have jaws to suck blood out of the insect. Some spiders are good and eat grasshoppers because grasshoppers are bad.

Here Katie made a connection to what she learned from another folder in which Jeff wrote about the devastation grasshoppers can cause to entire fields. Katie's final entry again referred back to *Charlotte's Web* when she editorialized on what she had just read:

> Spiders die before their babys hatch. And I think that is sad.

The investigative thinking extended out of school. Theron's entry in the earthworm folder is one example. He came in on a rainy April morning and wrote:

> On my way to school I saw a puddle. In the puddle I [saw] a worm this big. I thought a worm needed to live in dirt. But it was water. It looked like its skin was pulling off. Bye-Bye. The End.

Theron's writing led to class discussions and speculations of why we see worms in puddles, why they come out on rainy mornings. A couple of weeks later we found the beginnings of an answer when David reported reading that earthworms drink through their skin. Since earthworms also need air, the speculation went, they probably come up to get a drink and a breath of fresh air since it gets so muddy underground.

I saw more evidence that the children were taking their literacy outside of the classroom when we visited the new dinosaur exhibit at the Philadelphia Academy of Natural Sciences. Jon was one of the three boys in my group. He looked at a stuffed rhinoceros, commented that it resembled a dinosaur, and wondered if the rhinoceros evolved from the dinosaur. "Hmmm? How could you find out?" I asked. Jon smiled and without further prompting walked over to the attendant and asked. "No," came the answer, with an explanation that the dinosaur was a reptile and the rhinoceros is a mammal. Jon's reaction was not disappointment because of an incorrect hypothesis, but satisfaction that his thinking was clarified. When Jon saw a picture of a dinosaur with bright reds and oranges on its head he cried, "Look! There's *red* dinosaurs!" The curator explained to Jon a new theory in regard to dinosaur colors. As we walked away Jon commented, "Amanda was right. They could be any color!"

Conclusions

We continued writing, talking, questioning, sharing, and learning together. The children came to expect and rely on writing as a means of understanding their experiences. In a class discussion about the value of writing, Stephen put it this way: "It's good, it's hard to explain, but like you learned things and then you forgot and, when you write, you remember them again."

They also came to count on responses from the group, this *literate community*, to clarify their learning. On the last day of school, small groups sat around the room sharing writing from their China logs. As I walked around the room, I heard Mark reading to his peers: "Pandas like honey. They take honey from bees. Bees can't sting them because they have tough fur." Jared responded: "No, not tough skin. They have tough inside their mouths! Remember the film told us." Mark answered: "Oh yeah, that's right." (He stopped to make a change on his page.) "I wonder if they have tough skin too. Probably they do or they'd get stung on their fur. I could look it up."

The children had become thinkers and inquirers searching for meaning in *all* areas of the curriculum. The key element was transferring the components of our writing workshop to our studies in science, social studies, and math, and demonstrating to children that writing could be an important tool for all learning. Because children were familiar and comfortable with the workshop structure, they were able to move easily into this mode of learning in other subject areas. The writing became the primary tool in developing literacy.

The components of this literate environment were (1) chunks of class time for writing and thinking, (2) affirming responses and interactions with peers, (3) opportunity for revision and expansion of thinking and writing, and (4) individual ownership of learning. Underlying all of these components was my trust in these learners which encouraged risk taking.

The trusting environment allowed learners to take responsibility for their own learning, their own research. Toby Fulwiler has said that researchers become involved when they pose questions that they would really like to answer (Fulwiler 1985). I observed my students become responsible learners, taking ownership of their learning, when I allowed them to choose their topics and seek answers to their own questions.

What is the teacher's role? I found that, in addition to establishing the structure, it was important for me to provide books, media, and experiments of interest to the children and to encourage and listen to their questions. I also asked questions of them: Why do you think this?

How do you know? What does this mean to you? I found that children internalized these questions and then began asking the same questions of themselves and their peers. This nudged them to take on more responsibility for their learning processes. I also believe that it was important for me to be willing to be a learner *with* the children, writing with them, wondering, delighting in new awarenesses and realizing that it is not necessary to know all the answers in order to plunge into a topic. Above all, my trust in their capacity to learn enabled the children to take the necessary risks to plunge into new material, make mistakes, revise thinking, and develop new understandings.

Janet Emig (1983) has said that literacy is not worth teaching if it does not: provide access, sponsor learning, unleash literal power, and activate the greatest power of all—the imagination. Literacy develops when students use language to unleash their imaginations, discover meaning in all areas of the curriculum, and carry this process out of the classroom into all areas of their lives.

Stephen came to me in June and said, *"Now* I know why the space shuttle blew up. I've been listening to the news and I've been talking to my Dad and I saw a picture in the paper and I could read it too." Then he proceeded to draw a picture and explain O-rings to me. Stephen is literate.

References

Calkins, Lucy McCormick. *Lessons From a Child*. Portsmouth, NH: Heinemann Educational Books, 1983.

Dahl, Roald. *James and the Giant Peach*. New York: Knopf, 1961.

Emig, Janet. *The Web of Meaning: Essays on Writing, Teaching, Learning and Thinking*, edited by Dixie Goswami and Maureen Butler. Upper Montclair, NJ: Boynton/Cook, 1983.

Fulwiler, T. "Research Writing." In Mimi Schwartz (ed.), *Writing for Many Roles*. Upper Montclair, NJ: Boynton/Cook, 1985.

Fulwiler, T. "Writing and Learning, Grade Three." *Language Arts*, 62 (1985): 55–59.

Graves, Donald. Address at Millersville University, Millersville, PA, June 1986.

Graves, Donald. *Writing: Teachers and Children at Work*. Portsmouth, NJ: Heinemann Educational Books, 1983.

Kraus, Robert. *Leo the Late Bloomer*. New York: Thomas Crowell, 1971.

White, E. B. *Charlotte's Web*. New York: Harper, 1952.

[Language Arts *64, no. 6 (1987): 611–18*]

4

Literature

"What Did Leo Feed the Turtle?" and Other Nonliterary Questions

E. Wendy Saul

> I hate it when teachers ask skills questions. You want to do well so you redirect your reading to focus on those kinds of things. It's too insulting, and what's more, it spoils books.
>
> —Mary Posek, English major, recalling her precollege reading experiences

Through university courses in children's literature, reading, and language arts I teach that young people are best served by real books, conceived and written by authors who care about ideas and language. But privately I worry . . . if teachers don't know what to do with a book (and feel that they must do something) will they turn to the skills lists for questions and activities? In short, why is it that the questions my students plan to ask children following the reading of a story, poem, or novel sound like they were manufactured in basal land?

This paper is premised on two assumptions: first, that interpretation is key to literary comprehension, conversation, and enjoyment, even in the primary grades, and second, that skills instruction often takes away from literary discourse. At present there is considerable support in the schools for the marriage of literature and skills. This approach makes about as much sense as teaching painting by directing children to hold sticks and wave their hands up and down. Through my own classes I sought to examine how prospective teachers might better understand the importance of interpretive moves and become more adept at asking literary questions.

The work that I report here took place over four semesters. About two years ago I identified what seemed to be the problem: if students were unfamiliar with the pleasures of, and meanings evoked through, literary conversation, how could I expect them to appreciate the importance of making such talk part of classroom life? I, like most of my colleagues, saw the problem as conceptual. Students had too little experience reading and discussing books. Until they could distinguish between a literary discussion and a teacher-directed reading activity, I could not expect them to ask literary questions.

Teacher-directed reading questions were relatively easy to define. The categories are seemingly neat—main idea, detail, inference, sequencing, vocabulary, opinion—and apparently familiar to students who hadn't yet had a reading methods course. I assumed that these prospective teachers were attracted to reading skills questions, at least in part, because they knew what a reading skills question looked like. But literary conversation is more allusive. They needed examples. They needed models. They needed to experience the satisfaction of feeling how a work, through oral or written communication, becomes one's own.

My students are required to read widely in children's literature, but generally I lead class discussions. To help them better understand interpretation I sought a method which might make them more self-consciously literary in their thinking. I began by reading aloud Cynthia Rylant's (1985) well-crafted and moving story "Slower Than the Rest" which follows Leo, a ten-year-old boy who's been assigned to a class for "slow" children, as he finds and befriends a turtle he names Charles. During "Fire Prevention Week" Leo brings Charlie, a congenial turtle, to class as part of his presentation.

> "When somebody throws a match into a forest," Leo began, "he is a murderer. He kills trees and birds and animals. Some animals, like deer, are fast runners and they might escape. But other animals"—he lifted the cover off the box—"have no hope. They are too slow. They will die." He lifted Charlie out of the box. "It isn't fair," he said, as the class gasped and giggled at what they saw. "It isn't fair for the slow ones."
>
> Leo said much more. Mostly he talked about Charlie, explained what turtles are like, the things they enjoyed, what talents they possessed. He talked about Charlie the turtle and Charlie the friend, and what he said and how he said it made everyone in the class love turtles and hate forest fires. Leo's teacher had tears in her eyes.

Leo follows his class to the "Prevention Week" assembly and mentally drifts off. He is brought back suddenly by a classmate, "Leo, it's you . . . you won!" He had received a plaque for the best presentation in the school. As he shook the principal's hand ". . . he thought his heart would explode with happiness." The story concludes:

> That night, alone in his room, holding Charlie on his shoulder, Leo felt proud. And for the first time in a long time, Leo felt *fast*.

To see if I was correct in my assumptions about the students' literary orientation (or lack thereof) I asked them to list some questions they would ask children about this story. The majority of questions called upon students to rehearse the text, and could be answered with one or two words (although my guess is that children would be asked to write out answers in complete sentences).

—What type of animal was Charlie?

—Why was Charlie special to Leo?

—What happened to Leo that made him feel fast?

—What did Leo feed the turtle?

—How did Leo feel about himself before the award?

—How did Leo feel about himself after the award?

—How did Leo meet Charlie?

—What does "congenial" mean?

—What made Leo feel unhappy in school?

Another group of questions seemed almost independent of the text.

—Do you think that it is fair to label people?

—Have you ever had a pet?

—How would you feel if you had to be put in a special class for slow learners?

—Would you like to have a pet turtle? Why?

All the queries in group A could easily be marked right or wrong— these are what my students refer to as "fact" questions. The questions in group B are what students call "opinion questions"; here, any answer is welcome.

Finally there were two questions that might lead children into the story and help them consider the work as a human construction where craft and effect are taken seriously.

—Were Charlie and Leo alike in any way? How?

—What else could Leo have meant when he said "It isn't fair to the slow ones" during his presentation?

These questions seemed better—they were at once story-oriented and appropriately complex.

My next goal was to find a way to engage these preservice teachers in a literary discussion so that they could better appreciate its value. I wanted to model a teacher style which is at once active, accepting, and critical. I sought an approach which might invite even young children to see that literature can be discussed holistically. I looked for a situation in which there were no right and wrong answers, but where textual support for an interpretation would clearly be valued. Here it was: an idea I call "diagramming stories."

The purpose of this exercise is to find a shorthand way to focus on the structural peculiarities of a text, to comment on what in the book or story looms largest to the reader, and to describe, in something close to metaphorical terms, the essence of the book. Moreover, the diagram is seen only as the starting point of a conversation. It is important that we work on a blackboard with chalk. The diagram in this way becomes the visual analog of a conversation—transient but useful in, for instance, writing a paper or centering on a given text.

And my diagrams answer yet another problem—the dilemma of what to do with students who come to class believing that the task of people in literature is to unearth the bizarre in a text, to go where no reader has gone before. Mechanically they set about their business, seemingly untouched by the book, ready to pounce upon unsuspecting pupils with queries regarding hidden meaning. The beauty of the diagramming approach recommended here is that it is based largely on a naive reading of the work—it invites students to think about how a given tale is shaped, and how it has moved the reader. In short, there is no hiding behind literary devices.

I talked with students about interpretation, and had the framers of the questions cited above work together on a diagram on the blackboard. The original blackboard diagram began like most first attempts—a linear, chronological accounting of the tale. In this instance my student K. had Leo in a class with several other children. His mouth was down-turned. Another student suggested to K. that she make Leo's head square since everyone else in the diagram had round heads. K. thought that was a good idea. Then someone else suggested the possibility of steps to signify important changes in the rhythm of the story. Again there was erasing and discussion. It was at this point—when the discussion grew animated—that I asked students to begin work on their own interpretive drawings. I present three here, accompanied by the students' own (transcribed) comments as they introduced their representations to the class.

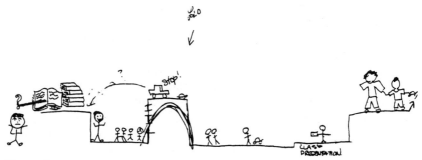

Figure 1.

I

I start out with Charlie with a stack of books and him being a little bit bewildered. And then he goes and takes a step down when he's put in special ed. He's in there with all the other children, he's the last one with a sad face. I don't know. He feels kind of out-of-place. And I had originally had this with a dotted line going up to a plateau where he's in the car and yells "stop" finding Charlie, but I decided instead it should only be more of a hill because it's only a temporary high. And he slides right back down where it levels off again, where there's other children.

Then there's only Leo and Charlie. Then I had a small step up when he gives the class presentation because he was excited about that. And it made him feel good. He wasn't real thrilled with what the other kids were saying, but I'm pretty sure he liked what he was saying.

And then, finally there's the principal and Leo and he's holding Charlie in his hand and that's a big step up because I think for once he feels faster.

And then, at the end I had little arrows going up because I think that this is just the beginning to where things are going to start moving faster and better for him as he gains more self-confidence.

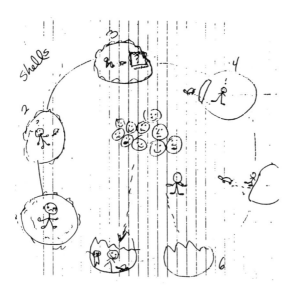

Figure 2.

II

Here I have Charlie inside of a shell himself and he's isolated, that's what the shell represents, and he's isolated from the people in the middle, OK?

And in the second shell, that's where he's met Charlie, you know, he's wondering "What is this?" And how do I relate to this animal in a shell also?

And then we have him up in the third shell and that's a window outside the shell and this is kind of like Charlie is looking out of the window also and he's observing things and he's getting Leo to look outside also.

Now there's Charlie walking outside the shell and he's showing Leo there's a way out. And Leo is real surprised and saying, "Maybe I can do that also."

And in #5 he follows Leo toward the group of people so Leo has a lot of curiosity and he wants to explore the world and things like that, and he's showing Charlie that there's no harm in going outside his shell.

In #6 of course he's outside his shell, it's shattered and he goes toward the crowd and he interacts with them like when he shares his experiences and his thoughts about the fire and his experiences with Leo.

And the arrow and the dots show him having returned to his shell again, he's got his little first prize award with him to the left and he's a happy little boy there in his shell. But the shell is now shattered and he can go in and out now and interact with people. So that's how I saw it.

Figure 3.

III

I've represented both Charlie and Leo as turtles. I didn't use any people and I made the rest of the people hares, rabbits. At the beginning Charlie was behind the rabbits, he was very slow and then he meets another turtle and they're both sort of moving along at the same pace. Then they start to fall in love with each other, they're just really fond of each other. Then he moves over and gives his presentation. And then all the hares fall in love with him and the turtle too and then they receive the award and all the hares are just sitting around looking at him and they're satisfied. Then at the end they're sort of in the same place as the hares.

I was very pleased. These interpretations were surely literary; students had struggled, productively, to say something significant about the story. And they knew that they had done well. Moreover, they had talked to one another and profited from the suggestionsof their peers. Smugly I again asked them to list a few questions for children, now that they better understood the nature of literary conversation.

With one exception (the woman who did the diagram about the shell) nothing changed. The second batch of questions was every bit as mechanical and uncritical and uninspired as the first.

I was puzzled. My only explanation was that they needed more time, that old habits die hard. But the students had been really impressed with each other's work. Why hadn't they, minimally, used the metaphors set up by their peers? Why had no one, for example, asked the children to compare the turtle in this story to the one in the "Tortoise and the Hare?"

Six months later . . .

I took the problem, much as you see it, to yet another group of students. I began with a discussion of the importance of literary conversation, and we examined questions from last term's class. This year's group, too, saw these queries as boring, mechanical, not the stuff from which literary understanding is born.

Then we moved to the three renderings cited above. My idea was that the points where the three interpretations differed might serve as a well from which to dip better questions. This happened before I anticipated it. One student, just after hearing the second explanation, noted, "Isn't it interesting how they all confuse Leo and Charlie? That might be a good question . . . Why?" Others agreed. "Why did Rylant give them these names?"

I had a definite sense that this class, composed largely of English majors, clearly understood what an interpretive move looked like. They were even able to generalize some of the characteristics of a literary question:

- It goes beyond what is in the text, but always comes back to it.
- The answer to the question could be argued intelligently either way.
- There are at least two good answers, either of which could help us with the story.
- The question should help us better understand the story.
- The question should view the work as a human construction and take seriously issues of craft.

Moreover, the questions asked in last term's class were clearly familiar to this year's group. One student commented:

> My son, he's in ninth grade, loves English this year, for the first time ever. But he tells me that it isn't really English, it's philosophy. His teacher asks what you are calling literary questions, but my son was so used to the other kind he doesn't even recognize this class as English.

The discussion began to shift. Their explanations suggested that the basal-type questions may have to do with some other, more powerful notion of curriculum.

> Teachers are looking for things they can correct.
>
> Teachers want to make sure that the kids have really read the book. We assume they can't be trusted. It also seems that we can't ask something significant until after we've . . . it's like we've got to separate out the tasks. Like in math, one kind of thing has to come before another.

It became clear that issues of teacher power and powerlessness may also complicate the issue of literary study.

But the influence of nonliterary concerns on literary matters is nowhere more clearly felt than in this statement which elicited much head nodding.

> But I can see that there's a safety net in those crummy questions. What happens if you get really introspective and very literary-minded and produce children who love English and love books, even in the lower grades, and then their achievement tests aren't great? And then you have everyone, parents and administrators, to contend with, and they all see it as your fault because your questions weren't like the ones on the test. Doing something different is a lot riskier.

They were right. Although one needs the conceptual under-standing and experience to write literary questions, the politics of schooling cannot be ignored. Was that threat to their perceived welfare what, in fact, made my previous group of students, usually so anxious to please, hold fast to the safety net of skill-driven questions? Again, a student summarizes this point:

> Maybe we just don't trust our own interpretations. Instead we rely on our ideas of what teachers are supposed to do. We're afraid to play in school and literary discussion is fun . . . Teaching is supposed to be serious business.

I thought we had it all figured out. Just to prove the point and so that we could all congratulate ourselves, I asked them to write good, literary questions about the Cynthia Voigt novels we had just read.

They began to work. They looked frustrated. And then Dine, in a state of utter agitation, raised her hand. "I want to know why they became friends, but can I say it that simply, or do I want to say 'What qualities did Izzy possess that attracted Rosamond to her?' "

There it was, the piece I was looking for. My students had taught me where the inadequate questions came from—the problem was conceptual, yes, and political, yes, but it was also rhetorical.

"Let's try it both ways," I suggested. We did. Stilted lists did not compare favorably to even a rambling struggle to articulate meaning.

Other students jumped in. "If I were talking to a friend, I'd say, 'Why are they friends? Why did it work?,' but I want to know if the second question might give kids some help in clearly listing traits."

I felt M. catch herself falling: "I preferred the question about what qualities because I thought it gave students a framework. If you're trying to move them in a literary direction, maybe we should give them some literary jargon."

Barbara disagreed, "What 'qualities,' what 'personality traits' makes it sound more psychological than literary." Many nods of agreement.

We talked a bit longer, about how jargon isn't jargon when the idea is a part of you, and about the importance of authentic language in eliciting authentic responses. Students volunteered, one after another: "I have a really good example of a bad question: 'What is the significance of Patrice's nationality in the story?' What I really want to ask is "Why is Patrice French when the story is set on the Eastern Shore?" There were many more examples—translations of formal language into teacher-owned language, "comfortable talk." An unusually quiet student summed it up: "If you asked someone your age these [stilted] questions, you'd be embarrassed. Why not be embarrassed asking them to kids?"

I thanked the students. The students thanked me. And we all walked out of class grateful to be engaged in a field that at least, on occasion, celebrates such exchanges.

I knew where to go from here—to the library for further conversation, for a lengthier and more disciplined discussion of the issues raised by my students. The ideas my students and I developed were not exactly new, but through our classroom discoveries they became "ours." This classroom research made scholarship once again fresh—philosophy and research had to be tested against experience, rather than vice versa.

Again, this year I find my students asking questions from basal land, but I understand their impulses more clearly and can, at least, help them practice an alternative: "How is the answer to the question you ask informed by the text?" "Why does that question interest you?" "Is that the way you would speak to someone whose ideas you respect?"

I wish to learn with my class, to see ourselves as a community with genuine, bothersome curiosities which drive us to conversations *and* books. Again, my student Mary says it best:

> I worry that I won't, that teachers don't, identify themselves as learners. You go through the educational system and you think you've collected all your credentials and you assume, or you've been invited to assume, I think quite erroneously, that you have the answers. And then you put yourself in the position of a teacher or a parent and you think you should share this knowledge or wisdom with children. Whereas, if you put yourself in the position of learning, continuous learning, learning from them and learning something about yourself, you're in a better position to teach.

Reference

Rylant, Cynthia. *Every Living Thing.* New York: Bradbury Press, 1985.

[Language Arts *66, no. 3 (1989): 295–303*]

5 Literature

Children's Response to Literature[1]

Janet Hickman

There are at least three things every teacher should know about children's response to literature. First, there are characteristic response patterns that change with age and developmental level. Second, response to literature doesn't always announce itself as such, but often comes in the guise of other school activities like writing or art. Third, better-formed or more highly developed responses can be nurtured, but it takes time.

For very young children, experiences with literature are more social than literary. In describing the interaction of mothers and infants in read-aloud sessions, Lamme (1984) has shown that babies vocalize, point, and touch their books, but the mothers' actions are a strong influence on their responsiveness. From Ninio and Bruner (1973) we have a description of toddlers and their mothers with picture books; again the primary focus is the exchange between mother and child. With increasing age, children's focus slips from the reading situation (though it still may have important effects) to the story itself. This can be illustrated by the teacher-father of three young children who asked them how they wanted to sit for their individual bedtime stories. The two-year-old wanted to be on his lap, between the arms that held the book. The five-year-old chose to sit beside him in the comfort of a one-arm hug. The seven-year-old opted for a companionable distance, side by side on the couch, close but not touching.

Preschoolers and early primary children are inclined to use their bodies as they respond; they wiggle and bounce and clap and echo story actions as they listen. When they talk about a book, they characteristically retell the story or supply a list of the characters (Applebee 1978). Applebee's older subjects began to summarize and categorize stories and finally, as they moved through adolescence, to analyze and generalize about literature. In middle childhood he found

---

[1]NCTE/CBC Series on Children, Writers, and Literature

a strong tendency to see personal response as an attribute of the story itself, i.e., if it doesn't interest me, it's a boring book; if I like it, it must be good. And the response that Squire (1964) identified as "happiness binding," the inclination to interpret a happy ending in spite of contrary evidence in the text, persists into adolescence.

The point of knowing something about these and other characteristic responses is that none of them should come as a surprise to the teacher. Children responding in age-approriate ways are not making "mistakes" or being difficult when they fail to see a story as an adult sees it. Rather, they are showing the level of response that comes most naturally to them; and that, of course, shows the teacher where to begin.

It would be easier to keep track of the impact of literature on children if their responses were always direct and immediate. However, part of what they think and feel often comes embedded in other activities.

I once watched a seven-year-old named Warren stare at a painting done by another child. It represented the storm-tossed ship of Spier's *Noah's Ark*, a book that I knew was already familiar to Warren. Shortly afterward he proceeded to paint his own picture of a storm at sea, on a much larger scale, and with a figure he identified as "Captain." Later he composed a story to accompany this picture.

The snowy story

The Captin is sailing a ship
that is woodin. Soon the
Captin ses "is There a storm
cuming up?" he said. The Captin
was right. There was a storm
wen the storm hit the sea the
moon is hidin in the fluding
sea. The man is fros solid.
The light house is looking
for the moon. The ship is creeking
The grol is foling out for the
ship. and they all ful in the
water. But the Captin didn't.

(Hickman 1980)

When Warren's mother came to collect him after school I mentioned that his writing held a real sense of poetry, and that I was reminded somehow of Longfellow's "The Wreck of the *Hesperus*." (I invite you to look up a copy and compare the two.) That poem, his mother said, was one that Warren had just happened to hear on a children's television program.

It would be too bad to think of Warren's work simply as "writing" and "art," because it also reveals a great deal about the impact of literature. We can see what drew the focus of his attention and how he was able to link powerful images from the picture book with similar material from the narrative poem. His work carries his response; it tells us more about his perception than a typical direct statement ("It was good") would have done. In situations where children are free to work with their own ideas, teachers will find good clues to their understanding of stories within many activities that are not labeled "literature."

When we learn to recognize children's response in all its forms, what then? It's the nature of school to demand progress and improvement, but such is the nature of response that it can't be directly taught. Teachers can, however, do much to encourage what Britton called "the improved response, the developed sense of form" (Britton 1968). One way is to implement his prescription for a combination of wide reading and close reading. This works in kindergarten as well as in upper grades if the teacher makes sure that students spend time with a variety of books, reads aloud daily from carefully selected titles, and pays special attention to some of these with much discussion, rereading, and extension activities. Under these circumstances children begin to make conscious links and connections. "This is just like the story you read to us yesterday." This is the sort of involvement that marks a reader of literature, even among those who haven't yet acquired the skills of reading.

Certainly the effects of wide reading and close reading on responses are cumulative, which is another way of saying that teachers must be patient, must allow time for the good things to happen. But they do happen. In one rural Ohio school a group of sixth graders meet regularly with their teacher for read-aloud and discussion sessions. Thanks to the structure of the school, most of them have been part of a similar group for three years. Now, nearing the end of this long chain of literature experiences, they are making shrewd connections and seeing beneath the surface of challenging material. When the book under discussion was Ursula LeGuin's fantasy, *A Wizard of Earthsea*, one of the boys drew on his own wide reading experiences and offered an observation that the teacher recorded in her journal:

> J. said that Ged in *Wizard*, Alison and Gwyn in *The Own Service*, David (and Keith) in *Earthfasts*, and Sybil in *The Forgotten Beasts of Eld* were all "drawn by something beyond their power to resist." He then proceeded to explain each situation. I cannot even begin to explain the sense of awakening that spread through all of us in the study group.*

---

*Quoted with the permission of Sheryl Reed, teacher, Ridgemont Elementary School, Mt. Victory, Ohio.

In the end it is this excitement, this sense of discovery, that we are after. We nurture response to literature not just to hear children begin to talk like critics, but to see them find this kind of satisfaction in their reading.

References

Applebee, Arthur N. *The Child's Concept of Story: Ages Two to Seventeen.* Chicago: University of Chicago Press, 1978.

Britton, James. "Response to Literature." In *The Dartmouth Seminar Papers: Response to Literature,* edited by James R. Squire. Urbana, Ill.: National Council of Teachers of English, 1968.

Garner, Alan. *The Own Service.* Walck, 1968.

Hickman, Janet. "Response to Literature in a School Environment." In *Oral and Written Language Development Research: Impact on the Schools.* Proceedings from the 1979 and 1980 IMPACT Conferences sponsored by the International Reading Association and the National Council of Teachers of English with support from the National Institute of Education.

Lamme, Linda. Paper presented at the 1984 convention of the International Reading Association. May, 1984.

LeGuin, Ursula. *A Wizard of Earthsea.* Parnassus, 1968.

Mayne, William. *Earthfasts.* Dutton, 1967.

McKillip, Patricia. *The Forgotten Beasts of Eld.* Atheneum, 1974.

Ninio, A., and Bruner, Jerome. "The Achievement and Antecedents of Labeling." *Journal of Child Language,* 5 (1973): 1–15.

Spier, Peter. *Noah's Ark.* Doubleday, 1977.

Squire, James R. *The Responses of Adolescents While Reading Four Short Stories.* Urbana, Ill.: National Council of Teachers of English, 1964.

[Language Arts 63, no. 2 (1986): 122–25]

6 *Drama*

Building Castles
in the Classroom

Karen L. Erickson

"Castles, is it?" The instructor, Mr. Jones, gets up, dons a hat, and speaks in a voice unlike his own. "I can tell you about castles. My name is Sean O'Casey and I own a castle. I've been wanting to sell the wretched thing and get it off my hands. It's costing me a great deal of money and now I'm even willing to give it away."

There is a shift in the room. The students seem to age and take on a strange air of maturity. They know they are being addressed as people other than themselves and they are waiting to find out who they are.

This morning, as these third grade students first walked into the class, they found themselves seated in a circle in the middle of the room. After a brief welcome by the instructor, the students were asked to introduce themselves. A catch in the proceedings was that they had to accompany their introduction with a gesture of some type that they thought might reflect the Middle Ages. Second, everyone in the class would imitate that gesture along with them. One by one, the students created flourishes with imaginary swords, cast spells, and curtsied before a baron as they introduced themselves. The rest of the class imitated each action after it was presented. The instructor asked them what they knew about the Middle Ages. The students tried to recall anything they might have heard or seen about the period. The one thing they spoke on with great authority was castles.

The instructor, still in character, continues. "How many of you would be willing to visit my castle and stay in it overnight?"

All hands go up.

He continues, "Well then, I'd be willing to give you the opportunity to stay the night and, if you do, I'll let you keep the castle in the morning."

A rush of excitement overtakes the students. They can't believe their ears. Again the hands go up. They are eager with their questions.

> *Students:* You say you'll give us the castle? All we have to do is stay the night?

Instructor: That's correct.

Students: All of us? We each get the castle? How can we do that?

Instructor: The castle ownership will be shared by everyone who stays the entire night and signs the record of deed the next morning. The specific evening you stay the night will have to be agreed on by the entire group.

Students: What's the catch?

Instructor: No catch. That's all you have to do.

Students: Where is this castle located?

Instructor: (makes a quick decision) Ireland.

Students: There's the catch then, how are we to get to Ireland?

Instructor: Are most of you without money for travel?

One or two say they have money but the rest admit they have little funds for travelling or their jobs won't allow them to travel. Most students are entering some adult role by this time.

Instructor: Well, then, I will pay the air fare of anyone who wants to participate but doesn't have the cost of the ticket. However, if you don't stay the entire night you have to give me my money back. Agreed?

They all agree enthusiastically.

Students: Why are you willing to pay all this money just to get someone to stay overnight in the castle, and then give it away? Is there something wrong with your castle?

Instructor: If there was something wrong with it, wouldn't I tell you? It is just an ordinary castle overlooking the sea, high on a hill.

Students: Then why are you going to spend all of this money?

Instructor: Because no one yet has stayed in the castle an entire night. Many say they will but then they don't.

Students: Is it true that people go into your castle and never come out?

Instructor: You've heard that! I've never known it to happen. Are you thinking you might turn down my offer?

Students: I don't know. I'm not sure I trust you.

Instructor: I'm not here to force anyone into staying in my castle who doesn't want to. I'm sure there are others here that would be willing to spend the night. The rest of you are ready to visit my castle, aren't you?

Faces become a little more complex. Fewer hands go up. There is something going on here and they are not so hasty to raise their hands.

Students: Is your castle haunted?

Instructor: I don't believe in ghosts. Do any of you believe in ghosts?

Hands go up. Funny, they all do.

Students: Is there a treasure buried in your castle?

Instructor: I've heard many stories about treasure, but I've never heard that the family buried one. I'll tell you what, if you stay the night in the castle, you can spend the time looking for the treasure. What you find is yours. It is a gift along with the castle.

Students: Do you have a map of your castle that we might look at before we make up our minds?

Instructor: (This question makes the instructor pause.) I think that can be arranged. Give me a week and I'll send to Ireland for maps.

The students all agree for they know a week in drama time is only a few minutes or hours or at the worst the next day. The instructor removes his hat and dismisses the students to music class. There they are introduced to some new music and they learn that for a few weeks they will be listening and studying music from the Middle Ages (hardly coincidental). Back in language arts class that afternoon the instructor puts back on his hat and greets the students in role as Sean O'Casey.

Instructor: Thank you all for coming back this week to our second meeting. It's wonderful so many of you returned. So, you're all still interested in the castle? I have sent for and received these wonderful maps. They give a layout of the castle and also give you a clue as to where a treasure might be buried if there is a treasure. Oh dear, I only have one map for every two people so you will have to share with someone else at the meeting.

The instructor hands out the maps to eager hands. The maps are on white paper neatly tied with colored ribbons. The students are asked to wait until everyone has their map before they open them. They are finally told to open their maps. The cries, the astonished looks, the confusion lets the instructor know his plan is working.

Students: These maps are blank. There's nothing on them.

Instructor: No. That can't be. I was assured that the proper maps were coming.

Students: They are blank. Take a look.

Instructor: You know they must have gotten erased going through the X-ray machines at O'Hare Airport. What bad luck.

The teacher removes his character costume and addresses the students as himself.

Instructor: You know it is terrible luck that all of the maps were erased and we do need them for our play. It just so happens I have found all of these books on castles and they are located all over the room. Why don't we make up the maps ourselves and help the castle owner out. Everyone can look at castles and draw up their own map indicating where the treasure is located.

The students can't wait. They are immediately on task researching castles, learning the names of the parts of the castles, learning to draw maps, creating legends for their maps and, of course, figuring a way to put the treasure on the map without making it too obvious.

This is the beginning of a wonderful unit on the Middle Ages. On the second day, the students, armed with their maps, are ready to face the challenge of the castle. But before they get a chance to go ahead, someone in the class questions the instructor about the ghost that was brought up the first day. The instructor, in role, admits there is a ghost and asks the students if they have an idea who the ghost might be. One student reveals he has heard it is the spirit of a dead Viking warrior.

Instructor: A dead Viking do you think?

The students all agree.

Instructor: I'll give you time in the library today to find out if a dead Viking would be haunting a castle in Ireland.

The time in the library is invigorating as excited students work together to find out if Vikings ever visited, invaded, or inhabited Ireland. The students, as well as the instructor, are amazed to learn about the great Viking invasions. They tell the instructor for certain they know it is a Viking ghost.

Back in the classroom, the instructor asks the students how they think a Viking ghost ended up haunting an Irish castle. But the instructor won't let them share their ideas; instead he says, "Wait a moment, I have an idea. Don't tell me about the Viking legend . . . let's prepare to show Sean O'Casey the legend of his castle by acting those legends out." There is a burst of applause. The instructor immediately divides the class into groups of three or four and gives them the time to create a story on the Viking legend of the castle. During the next three days, as the students prepare their dramatizations, the teacher shows them a filmstrip on the Middle Ages and conquering nations; they begin to study the structure of legends and how they came to be written; they also focus on creative ways to dramatize ghosts so they aren't played the same as living people, enact death scenes without losing concentration, and move from location to location within the story without having to change sets.

In the first three days of school, the students have learned vocabulary of the Middle Ages, studied in detail some historical aspects of the Middle Ages, studied the characteristics of legends, written a legend with a group, practiced map making, participated in a highly sophisticated questioning process, and learned some new aspects in dramatizing stories. Every student was involved because the interest level was high. Drama was the significant unifying thread.

This unit of study and many more like it are taking place every day in the Glencoe Public Schools, Glencoe, Illinois. Supported by the administration, drama and the other fine arts have become powerful aids to the classroom teachers in presenting material from all curricular areas. When specialists aren't available as a resource because of funds, training is available to classroom teachers interested in the program so that they can carry out the program. It is a true measure of success that the idea of bringing drama into this school was first conceived of by a principal, but it is the classroom teachers' commitment to the program and their belief in the impact that drama has on learning that makes this program unique in the state of Illinois.

Drama is an organized exploration into self-awareness, human behavior, and self-expression using movement, rhythm, verbalization, sound and role playing. Drama in an educational environment becomes an art process based on play that allows students to explore, discover, talk about, deal with, accept, reject, and understand this complex world. It creates an environment that allows the participant to safely explore his or her own feelings, behavior, and ideas. Students learn to create new perspectives from familiar actions, stretch the imagination, and share experiences that work as a springboard to group interaction and cooperation. Drama is a natural process through which human beings can explore and expand their own ideas and potential while exploring the arts. The drama program in Glencoe is twofold: (1) to introduce students to drama and creative expression through movement, verbalization, and role-playing, and (2) to provide teachers with an in-depth look at a creative process through which they can stimulate learning in a variety of curricular areas.

Here I think it is important to share a few facts about the drama lesson on the Middle Ages.

1. The students in this class have been involved in classroom dramas since 1983. That is the year the program began. At the start of their fourth-grade year, they possess basic skills in

concentration, characterization, imitation, and imagination, movement, and verbalization. They know how to create dramas in a group, they have skills in listening, compromising, social interaction, and sharing. Teachers in the upper grades only need to give clues for dramas to begin. Throughout the drama play they work on additional performing arts skills along with the curricular content of the subject matter they are teaching. Younger children need to first learn basic skills so they too can begin work in full classroom dramas. The district is developing a sequential drama curriculum for the staff so that all teachers can actively aid in the drama process while having this teaching strategy available at their fingertips.

2. Not everything in this lesson was preplanned by the teacher. The instructor knew he wanted the children to learn the parts of a castle and the vocabulary of castles. The teacher wanted the students to become familiar with researching topics in the library. The teacher wanted to focus on legends and how legends are written, and he wanted to give the students a sense of the Middle Ages. In drama the teacher's goals included work on beginning, middle, and end in stories; concentration; characterization; and the smooth movement from one setting to another within the play. Mapmaking, the Vikings' invasion of Ireland, and the hidden treasure were all the students' devices. The teacher knew how to blend his goals with that of the imagination of the students. Listening and compromise were the keys to the teacher's success.

3. Notice that, in the lesson, besides the curricular content, there were also art process skills being developed. The teacher's plans included artistic growth as well as language arts and social studies.

4. The questioning process recounted for you above is actually much shorter than the real work done in class. The questioning was not preplanned and the teacher had to use good listening skills to pick up ideas introduced by the students.

Major units of study in Glencoe incorporating drama as a learning medium include Indians, Explorers, Fairy Tales, Fables, Japan, Eskimos, the Chicago Fire, Nursery Rhymes, Tall Tales, Animals (many different units), Greece, Farm Life, Trees, Butterflies, Rome, Creative Writing, Color and Light, Outer Space, Planets, and the Circus.

If we want students to become experts on subjects, the key is involvement. You become good at what you do only by becoming totally immersed in it. We know that play can totally immerse children. Their involvement can become so real that pretending loses all meaning. Children can find sheer joy in learning through play. As we grow up, we lose this ability to become totally involved and immersed in our work or in our hobbies. Exposure to the arts and to play can once again renew our ability to achieve expert status. Drama, because it is so closely akin to play, immediately draws children in, enlisting the senses and the entire physical nature of the human being to awaken *all* the functions of the mind. With their minds awakened, children increase their power to learn, and their chances of becoming experts. The arts are the connecting links that can involve students creatively in their own learning and help them see the interrelation of *all* knowledge.

Children play at castles on the playground. For hours, they fight battles and search for treasure. But in the classroom, in units of study on castles, where teachers do not have a method to tap into a child's ability to play, a student will usually only read information from a text, memorize vocabulary, take tests, and write the essay on castle life. Something is lost to this student. That teacher who can make the castle live through drama in the classroom has tapped the rich resources of the student's imagination to totally involve the entire human being in the learning process. It is the child involved in the second teaching method that really learns, remembers, and comes to understand the material. Drama is the learning medium. Drama makes castles in the sky a reality in the classroom.

[Language Arts *65, no. 1 (1988): 14–19*]

Storytelling

Connecting to Language through Story

Marni Schwartz

Just before I began to write this article, I stopped by a well-stocked music store and bought an Easy-to-Play book of Gershwin tunes I had seen in the window. I haven't played the piano much since I gave up lessons at age fourteen. At that time I offered the excuse that cheerleading, chorus, and swim team took all my time. Actually, an overwhelming sense of inadequacy as I faced the piano and my teacher moved me to quit.

I wasn't a kid who lacked self-esteem. In cheerleading my backjump arch ranked among the best on our team. The chorus director acknowledged my ability by moving shaky second sopranos to sing near me. At swim meets my dives could guarantee a few team points because I'd been diving with a coach since I was old enough to say, "One, two, three, spring up." In these areas I was self-assured. But at the piano, faced with my assigned pieces, I was a loser.

Every September when I ask students to introduce themselves to me in writing, more than a few state, "I'm no good in English." They have undoubtedly experienced that feeling of failure so familiar to me at the piano. Whether their embarrassment is a result of problems with reading, writing, filling in worksheets on parts of speech, or putting periods and commas in the right places doesn't matter. I know that I must help them connect to language personally and positively before they can begin to face the work of learning the processes and conventions of English.

Unfortunately these children have not often or ever seen themselves as powerful users of language. They see language as a right/wrong proposition. They believe there is a right way to read or a wrong way to write. (Ironically, when I teach adults, many of whom are language teachers, I find an equal percentage who believe they are "not good" at writing, speaking publicly, or performing dramatically for their peers.) I want to expose all my students to the exhilarating feeling of what it is to use language powerfully. I know every one of them can. Part of our job as teachers is to help our students realize they too can be masterful writers, speakers, readers, or performers. One device for building self-esteem in language class is storytelling.

Within the story experiences of people's lives is one secret to their connection with language. They have a well of story memories from which to draw. By dipping into this well they discover their long and often intense relationship with language. Through listening to stories they will deepen the well. In telling their own stories, they will experience some of the power of language, their language, be it natural or "borrowed."

Drawing from the Well

Many teachers encourage students to talk and write about meaningful life events. Some of those events are what I call story memories. We all possess memories of stories we've heard or read or watched. Story memories also include the times we told or read stories to others. In exploring those memories we "touch magic" (Yolen 1981).

I was first engulfed by my own story memories at a weekend gathering of storytellers and folkmusicians at the Sagamore Conference Center in the Adirondacks. Al Booth, a devotee of the poet Robert Service, had driven all the way from Maryland just to satisfy the need for song and story. I'll never forget how he brought to life the stranger "who looked to me like a man who'd lived in hell" and the shooting of Dan McGrew. Later, at the request of those who'd heard the narrative poems before, he told of the "strange things done in the midnight sun by the men who moil for gold." He cremated Sam McGee right before our eyes. Hearing the musical rhythms of the narrative poems brought me back to two I'd memorized in high school but since forgotten. Al's recitals challenged me to work on one of those the rest of the weekend. Now I consider Stephen Vincent Benét's "The Mountain Whippoor-will" a treasured object I'll be careful not to lose again.

Two other tellers, a couple who perform under the title Beauty and the Beast, took on the characters of Very Tall Mouse and Very Short Mouse from Arnold Lobel's *Mouse Tales*. Both the story and the friendship they obviously shared awakened memories of laughing over Frog and Toad's antics with my son.

Through the weekend workshops I began to take my turns recalling poems, songs, or short anecdotes about stories from my past. What helped me recollect bits and pieces of my "story history" were the tales or memories others shared. One woman's A. A. Milne poems brought back Piglet's pretending to be Roo. I still shudder at the thought of Kanga approaching Piglet with a spoon of medicine meant for the little kangaroo. The more poems I heard, the more I remembered. The funny rhymes of Laura E. Richards' "Eletelephony" came flooding back. My mother always looked humorously forlorn when she cried, "Dear me! I am not certain quite that even now I've got it right." I almost recalled the entire "When in disgrace with fortune and men's eyes . . ." a sonnet whose recital had brought me extra credit in sophomore English. With a little help from Sagamore's library I was able to do both Shakespeare and Miss Butler proud. What surprised me again and again over the weekend was how we triggered each other's stories. Every participant was empowered to say, "I have a story."

Now as I use storytelling in the classroom, I spend significant time asking students to search their pasts for story memories. These can relate to books someone read to them or they read on their own. The memories can include family stories or tales from cassette tapes, the radio, movies, or TV. I make a point not to discount the source of any story memory. It's a case of the haves and have nots if I recognize only book titles. Yet, it is an easy place to start. *Mike Mulligan and his Steam Shovel, The Cat in the Hat, The Pokey Little Puppy,* and of course countless titles I've never heard of come pouring out. I'm always struck by the shouts of "Oh yeah, I remember that one" which validate a recollection. Story memories abound.

I encourage the stories behind the stories (the tales' tails?). I tell how I learned "The Mountain Whippoorwill" under duress. As a cocky ninth grader I imagined the drama coach, Mr. Quirk, was having a nervous breakdown because he wanted us to do a choral reading. They tell how they memorized a story in order to "read" it to a younger sibling or doll. Then others chuckle at the memory of believing they had fooled their parents by such "pretend" reading. Still others recall the applause of proud grandparents or remember special tales associated with a great- aunt's lap or her childhood. Some tell of adults who chronicled nightly the lives of imaginary characters. David told of his father's original stories in which Davey was the hero. Later, when each of the children worked on a story for a polished telling, David took the role of his dad and let us in on the magic he must have experienced as a child hero. In every case the children's recountings elicit other stories. I've felt on occasion as if I'm in the middle of a fabulous "jam session" of tellers.

I believe this rich history is the place to begin to introduce children to storytelling. It is a deep well which children can return to again and again once they realize it's there.

Something different happens when children prepare a story, work on it, as they would work on a piece of writing. I am careful not to discount the stories that have emerged naturally. Powerful, spontaneous oral language is highly regarded in our world. So is a well-crafted speech. By practicing a story, seeing it change and grow, and telling it before an audience, children experience a special kind of thrill. Anyone who has run a school play or starred in a backyard extravaganza knows the magic of the stage. But it's more than just that. Actors are assigned roles. But storytellers find their stories, the ones they must tell. Then they make them their own.

Finding the Right Story

Some children dip right into the well of stories they already own and find one they must retrieve for a practiced telling. Others explore stories they have encountered only recently. Still others get hooked on the excitement of hunting for a treasure among the stacks or on records and tapes. What the teacher can provide is a variety of models and the time children need to choose well.

For students to see themselves as tellers, they must have good models. Naturally, the teacher must demonstrate. I tell of the church organist, Mrs. Burchim, who singled me out in the fourth grade to substitute for her as singer of the morning Mass. It's a personal tale I've worked on for two years, one that has a mind of its own. Each time the audience greatly affects the telling. Then I might tell Aesop's "Wind and the Sun," a simple fable that remains slightly more stable. If possible, I bring in student tellers from the previous year to continue to show the possibilities in story choice and storytelling style. They give testimony to the fact that choosing the right story is half the work. They talk about how they decided on a story to tell and problems they encountered and solved. Local tellers offer a special treat too. Our area contains folklorists rich in knowledge of the Iroquois, the Erie Canal builders and the folk of the Adirondack Mountains as well as the history of storytelling as an art. Commercial records, cassettes, and videotapes add to our source of models and stories as well.

Finally comes the choosing of a story to tell. At first, children choose stories by pictures, by title, or by a desire to recreate a story they've heard. Eventually, they dig with a more complex set of expectations. A story must touch them; it must satisfy their peers; it must not contain elements that confuse or distract them. Naomi switched from story to story. Her choices all seemed like good possibilities. She had little difficulty recalling story events. But none of the stories was "just right." Choosing a writing topic was often difficult for Naomi too. She would false-start, as a swimmer might, again and again. Like a starting judge, I'd want to disqualify her. But in recent years I've come to respect the wait time writers and storytellers need, painful as it can be for their teacher. When Naomi finally performed *The Snow Child*, I could see that her deep love for the story helped her bring it to life. Not one of the others had held her attention so completely. I believe Naomi made a significant decision by holding off. In waiting for her, I acknowledged her right to decide and offered her a chance to experience the power of the "right" story.

When some budding tellers hunt for a story they go to the films or television shows they have loved. While I believe much of TV weakens children's ability to visualize, I do not devalue the powerful emotional impact of stories from the media. Marla reminded me of the mark *Bambi* had left on my life. When she first asked to prepare that story for a performance, I tried to steer her away. She seemed to have only a vague recollection of the characters and events from the Disney movie. I suggested she find a text of it in order to get the order of events and more detail. We discovered together that the original *Bambi* was no easy text. Marla was not deterred. Her final telling brought the thicket, the owl, Thumper and the giggly ice-walking scene to life. When she whispered, "Fire!" you could feel danger hovering above the room. Then Bambi's mother was dead. Every listener seemed mesmerized by the beauty and the pain of Marla's story. I know I was.

Other media-versions have surfaced in my classroom. Some children know Jason and the Argonauts or Thor only through the big screen. I overheard Cliff and Rob arguing about exactly what happened to Medusa in a film they had seen. I directed them to various written versions of Perseus' tale so they could fashion a telling that fit them. Tellers have to try on several sizes of a story sometimes, and the movie version might be just a bit too big *or* too small.

Illustrations bring students to stories as well. Steve, a talented artist himself, wanted to tell Mercer Mayer's *Professor Wormbog's Gloomy Kerploppus*. His dad had read it to him many times, and Steve really admired the book's funny illustrations. When I suggested a storyboard as one exercise for learning a story, Steve dived into a masterful reproduction of Mayer's work. He spent several hours one night on the large storyboard. I originally hoped the activity would help students visualize a story's events rather than memorize its words. However, Steve seemed as reliant on his drawings to remember story events as did some of those groping for lovely but forgotten phrases. On the day of his performance for the class, Steve begged to have the storyboard in sight. My initial reaction was, "No, absolutely not," but as I learn repeatedly in working with children's language, there are no absolutes. I granted the request, and Steve gave a side-splitting, though somewhat choppy, performance of Mayer's work. Afterward, I asked Steve what he'd learned in the telling. He said he'd enjoyed working on the detailed drawing (he planned to give it to his dad for Father's Day), and he wanted to tell the story again without his cue card.

Learning by Telling

The most empowering part of storytelling lies not in the recollecting or learning but in the sharing. While I have used the terms "perform" and "tell" interchangeably, the two can differ in the act of sharing. A story is a gift from teller to listener. Tellers look into the eyes of the audience and what they see there affects their tone of voice, their facial expressions, their posture, even their words. Kristyn told her thirteen-year-old peers Dr. Seuss's *Yertle the Turtle*. Kristyn, admired by staff and students alike for her mature approach to life, delivered the story in a very adult way. Atop the pile of turtles, she surveyed the pond below from a great distance. So I sent her to a recreation program for kids in the four to six age range. How the telling changed! Her face softened; her eyes widened; she stooped to pull the kids closer to the excitement. She added lines like, "And do you know what happened next?" She seemed to discover the hunger for story in a group of young language users, and she didn't disappoint them. Later, we marveled at what had happened. We listened to the tape of her telling, and she laughed and laughed. I knew the child in her was alive and well and would continue to inform the adult.

Children can retell stories from a very young age. At a family reunion recently I was asked to "settle the kids down" before a bedtime that was already much too late for most of them. As the children got word that someone was telling stories, I sat on the front porch of my mother's house asking the few who had already arrived what stories they knew. Billy, age five, announced his favorite. With very little effort I drew him into the telling.

"I know *Where the Wild Things Are*."

"Oh, yes, I've heard that. What's the boy's name again?"

"Max. It's about when Max put on his wolf suit and went to where the wild things live."

"Oh, now I'm remembering. Billy, could you tell us that story?"

I took the role of crowd controller and settled the overtired crew as best I could. Once Billy knew he had the stage, a masterful look came over his face. I don't think he had ever known the attention of so many people before. At first he directed the tale only to me, but soon he "roared their terrible roars and smashed (gnashed) their terrible teeth" toward the entire crowd of adults and children now seated around him. He told the story almost word for word. Sendak's language and his tale of the boy's journey, his reign, and the sweet return home now truly belonged to Billy. Later, his mother said she had read the book to Billy perhaps twice over a year ago. She marveled that he'd internalized it so, but she acknowledged how much the story reflected Billy's struggle with behavior and need for approval. At five, Billy was closely connected to language.

Billy's learning of Sendak's words happened naturally. For children or anyone to learn a story successfully, the words must not get in the way. I encourage children to "draft" a telling much as they would a piece of writing, experimenting with intros, openings, and endings. They try out their stories with dialogue and without. Most importantly they work on visualizing the tale. If they can walk from scene to scene mentally, the words will come. Joanna had rehearsed her story many times for a partner or a small group. I could tell she had memorized the writer's phrasing. When she stood before the class, she panicked after about three lines. "I can't remember the words!" she gasped. "Just tell what happened next," I whispered. She started again. I could see her relax as she found the familiar characters and objects: Boots and his brothers hiking through the woods, the magic axe, the spade, and the trickling nut. At two other moments she began to lose concentration. I watched her fight off the distraction of her nervousness and return to the world of the story. At the end, she rolled her eyes, grinned, and sighed. Like Boots, who had heeded the calls of the powerful objects, Joanna had listened to the story in her mind and been rewarded.

Both children and adults choose certain stories because they must. Jane Yolen says, "Myth as serious statement plays an important role in the life of the child. It can be the child's key to understanding his or her own experience. It can also be the key to our understanding of the child." Gautham listed *Curious George Wins a Medal* on a sign-up list for possible stories. Now, Gautham had not exactly set my classroom on fire with energy the year he resided in my sixth grade. His writing came ever so slowly, his handwriting was truly indecipherable, and often, when questioned about an assigned task, he responded with a rather vacant grin. His parents and older brother had emigrated from India years before, but Gautham, born and bred in Schenectady, seemed the "typical American kid." Because the story's humor relies so much on the pictures of George's antics, I warned Gautham he'd have to work hard to help us see the story. Not all of us had story memories of the Curious George books to draw from.

I don't believe it was the warning that inspired the work Gautham put into the story's preparation. Over the next few days as I moved from teller to teller, watching and coaching, Gautham "told" his story to the wall, to the mirror, to boxes stacked on a corner. Usually very social, he chose to work alone during most of the rehearsal time. I didn't watch too closely for fear of distracting him. As is unfortunately the case, I'm often negligent of the students "on task" in order to help the less-involved. So when Gautham shared his version of Curious George, I saw it for the first time. What must have fueled the energetic rehearsals was his love of the story and his delight at the thought of sharing it.

To see George the monkey come to life is probably the fantasy of any child who has known him. Curious George really is a child— sensitive, clownlike, desperate to learn and explore, desirous to please but awkward in the attempt. Gautham became George, to the delight of every child (twelve or otherwise) in the room. We could see soap bubbles filling the house as George attempted to clean the spilled ink. We watched him get butted by a goat, stampeded by a penful of pigs, and chased by a furious farmer. When George's escape took him to the science museum, we groaned knowing the dinosaur skeleton so tall, but not so sturdy, would topple as George made his way to the familiar-looking coconut tree.

Gautham took George on the road to library storyhours and to some fifth grade classes. His performance made him famous throughout our school just as George's eventual ride in space earned him a medal. More importantly, his sharing of the story introduced me to a child I really had not known before. Gautham, like George, had roots in another world. Being born in America did not erase those roots though I think Gautham wanted very much to be connected to life American-style. He had not yet found his place in school except as it related to chatting with friends which often got him in trouble. Like many children he had not connected the richness of his experience to what school required of him.

My "school" piano memories never offered me a treasure I could retrieve when I sat down to play either. I had only frustrations or minor successes at the strange, unreal pieces from my piano books. But memories of "Fascinating Rhythm" from a cocktail piano record my mother bought when I was a child did awaken my desire to play. Just seeing the name Gershwin on an Easy-to-Play collection hurled me back to the smells in our kitchen and the memory of my father dancing me around as my mother prepared supper. That record played nearly every night during the dinner hour until it wore out or till my teenaged brothers convinced my mother they couldn't "listen to that stuff all the time." That memory, tucked away in the secret part of me that is invincible, yet is child, allowed me to stop in the music store and buy my first piano book in years. If we can teach children, allow them really, to explore and savor their indestructible pasts, we will empower them not only as language users but as people ever growing, ever wanting to learn.

References

Richards, L. "Eletelephony." In *The Random House Book of Poetry for Children*, compiled by Jack Prelutsky. New York: Random House, 1983.
Service, R. *Best Tales of the Yukon*. Philadelphia: Running Press, 1983.
Yolen, J. *Touch Magic*. New York: Philomel Books, 1981.

[Language Arts *64, no. 6 (1987): 603–10*]

8 *Storytelling*

Storytelling and Science

Kathleen Martin and Etta Miller

On a Saturday in late October two dozen seven- and eight-year- olds taught me how to teach science to young children. Prior to that revealing morning, my experiences with science teaching had been restricted primarily to high school. Not knowing where to begin my astronomy lesson proved to be a happy circumstance. I was forced to ask the youngsters what they already knew about space, stars, planets, and the like. My young scholars were in places I had not imagined. Black holes were of foremost interest with the question of life on other planets a close second. I found their naive sophistication delightful and their curiosity challenging.

As we pursued the question of whether Mars might have once sustained life, an argument ensued regarding the number of moons circling the planet. I recall with relief that their logic did not necessarily parallel their enthusiasm. Yet I found it exhilarating that seven- and eight-year-olds should experience persistent questions about such provocative and complex phenomena as black holes and life on other planets.

Listening to the arguments for three Mars moons versus two, I heard nothing which led me to believe that one child was thinking about the situation any more than the other. Therefore, I felt it unfair to resolve the argument simply by pulling rank and testifying to the fact that Mars did indeed have two moons. Instead I told the children that I would relate a story which might provide a clue to the correct answer. Drawing upon my store of mythology, I shared the story of the bloody battles of the Roman god of war and his two loyal sons, Diemos and Phobos, who always fought at their father's side. When I asked the children who knew the clue, a chorus of hands went up. Mars did indeed have two moons and their names were Diemos and Phobos.

The anecdote demonstrates the need for presenting science to children in a way that helps them to make associations and to see relationships among the facts they are studying. Children have a natural inclination to animate the world in order that they may more easily bring their own experiences to bear upon it. Ancient peoples felt a similar need to intertwine psychological life with their observations of physical phenomena. Mythology arose as a natural response to their observations of the heavens. Just as the Roman god Mars shared an affinity for his sons, so did the planet share an affinity for its moons.

We frequently forget that science is a story. Rather we fall into what Malcolm Weiss (1980) terms the "Madison Avenue view" of science:

> Science is true. Science is certain. Scientists are detached, objective observers. They follow in Mother Nature's footsteps murmuring, "Just give us the facts, ma'am" and from the facts they arrive, step by logical step, at clear and precise theories. Only on such things as TV commercials for headache remedies do "scientists" in white lab coats dole out Truth and Certainty.

The scientist seeks more than isolated facts from Mother Nature. The scientist seeks a story. Inevitably the story is characterized by mystery. Since the world does not yield its secrets easily, the scientist must be a careful and persistent observer. The story is never revealed to those who are unwilling to wait or to those who are not watchful.

What role do educators play in preparing children to participate in the story of science? Perhaps the first responsibility is that the educators themselves must come to a fuller understanding of science as a story. Traditional school science has been presented more in an expository mode than a narrative mode. Exposition is a kind of discourse which conveys information and explains that which is difficult to understand as though understanding were a mere matter of logic. It connotes an authority characterized by power—those who know telling those who are in need of knowing. Narration, on the other hand, is a detailed account of an event, the story of how the event unfolds. The authority of the storyteller resides in a keenness of observation and a sensitivity to significant moments.

The etymology of the word "story" reminds us that it is related to the Greek *eidos* which means the idea, form, or shape of things. Stories help us give shape and form to experience. A story acts as a container, thereby enabling the listener to discern how the diverse elements of an event or series of events are held together. Stories are as concerned with the connections between things as with the things themselves. The mythological story of Mars offers children a meaningful connection between the planet and its moons.

Story is also kin to the term "guise," which refers to the manner or appearance of things. People who are close to nature, such as farmers and sailors, attend carefully to the world's changing appearance; they are alert to the ways in which the world disguises itself. This attention invites storytelling, and these stories have come to constitute a whole body of literature known as weatherlore.

As any classroom teacher will attest, sudden shifts in weather are immediately manifest in the behavior of children. Their senses are particularly attuned to the subtle atmospheric changes heralding the more dramatic arrival of thunderstorms and other forceful meteorological events. Just as children's bodies respond to weather phenomena, so can their minds and imaginations.

> Birds flying high;
> The weather will be dry.
> Birds flying near the ground;
> Soon you'll hear the thunder's sound.

Weatherlore invites children to look at the world more carefully and, thereby, to ascertain the extent to which their observations are accurately reflected in the lore. For children, observation is at the heart of science. Stories, even very brief weather stories, can prompt observation. If, as in the case of high flying birds and dry weather, the observations seem to confirm the story, then children frequently seek elaboration. A child might conjecture that the thunder's sound drives birds near the ground to seek the shelter of trees. If, however, that same child attempts to test this hypothesis by producing thunderous sounds in the presence of birds, she or he will probably note that they take immediate flight. This story must then undergo revision. After further observations and any number of revisions and, perhaps, even a survey of the literature (reading more weather books), that child might eventually draw a series of connections between thunder and moisture, insects and birds, and begin to weave a story: Before the coming of a storm, humidity increases. Rising moisture easily weights the wings of high-flying insects. In search of relief they move nearer the ground with their feathered friends in hot pursuit.

If we teach children to observe the world with patience and care, then we must also teach them that watching and waiting is worthwhile. This is conveyed when they can make sense of events through a connecting story and can then delight in the relationships which they discover.

In suggesting that narrative is the most appropriate mode for exposing children to science, I would emphasize that the scientific story is a distinctive one. That distinction, however, cannot be reduced to simplistic separations such as the one between fact and fiction. Indeed, it is the transition from fact to fiction and vice versa which is, perhaps, more characteristic of science than either one. As new technologies are made available to scientists, the facts of today frequently become the fictions of tomorrow. Science is alert to change. Its language reflects this sensitivity in the dynamics of evolution and metamorphosis in biology, transitory states in chemistry and the Uncertainty Principle in physics.

Richard Feynman (1968) describes science as a process of questioning the experts. We think of the experts as those who have the facts. He warns:

> Each generation that discovers something from its experience must pass that on, but it must pass that on with a delicate balance of respect and disrespect, so that the race does not inflict its errors too rigidly on its youth, but it does pass on the accumulated wisdom, plus the wisdom that it may not be wisdom.

The "accumulated wisdom" of the race represents what a given people within a given time understand about their world and how it works. Such wisdom constitutes a way of seeing the world and, consequently, guides the interpretation of events. Etymology again becomes significant, for it relates the word "story" to wisdom. The scientific story, then, can be thought of as a kind of wisdom which enables us to hear among the facts of the world connections which the isolated facts do not convey. Feynman illustrates such wisdom in this story:

> Trees are made of air primarily. When they are burned, they go back to air, and in the flaming heat is released the flaming heat of the sun which was bound in to convert the air into tree, and in the ash is the small remnant of the part which did not come from air that came from the solid earth instead.

To the child who asks what trees are made of, this story constitutes a response far more powerful than the simple factual response that trees are made of cellulose. In the tree, earth and air are bound together through the heat of the sun. When the children who are inspired by this story grow older and begin to wonder about chemical composition and chemical change, cellulose takes on a meaning that extends beyond a mere name.

Storytelling is the oldest mode of teaching. Strangely enough, it may be the mode best suited to the newest discoveries in science. A good story honors the role of the storyteller, recognizing that the perspective of the storyteller has much to do with how the story is told. The history of science is very much a story of changing perspectives. For almost one thousand years the Aristotelian storyteller stood on a still earth at the center of the universe and spun tales about the worlds that moved harmoniously around him. Then in the middle of the sixteenth century the Copernican story was told, a perspective that shifted the sun to the center of the universe. The tale told by Copernicus was indeed earthshaking in that the newly perceived movement of the earth was a revolution in every sense of the word.

The Copernican story, however, still contained remnants of the old Aristotelian tale. In attempting to save the perfect circles which Plato and Aristotle ascribed to the heavens, Copernicus bequeathed us a story that still left the motions of bodies on earth separate from the motions of heavenly bodies. The combined geniuses of Kepler, Galileo, and Newton synthesized those motions through the image of a mechanical universe, every aspect of which was governed by the same mathematical laws. Newton's story, his explanation of how observations of the heavens and the earth fit together, was so powerful that it focused science into a singular perspective for almost three hundred years. In the twentieth century Albert Einstein emerged to deliteralize the Newtonian story with his own story of relativity. Since Einstein, the role of the observer has become increasingly significant.

In science the observer serves as the storyteller. Science, however, has tended to speak of theories, rather than stories. Perhaps the two are not so different. The word theory derives from the Greek *theos,* which refers to the playground of the gods. Playgrounds invite play, and theories, like stories, involve a play of images. Just as stories undergo change when told by a different storyteller, so do scientific theories change with the theorist. Aristotle, Copernicus, Kepler, Galileo, Newton, and Einstein all saw the world through different images and, consequently, constructed different stories about how the world works. While respecting the stories of old, each storyteller felt compelled to renew those stories through his own experience, to modify the stories or, perhaps, to even abandon them and to launch into the telling of an entirely new story. Feynman draws an analogy with science: "And that is what science is—the result of the discovery that it is worthwhile rechecking by new direct experience, and not necessarily trusting the race experience from the past."

In thinking about the young scholars who prompted the writing of this essay, I cannot but wonder if black holes and the question of life on other planets are inherently more interesting to them than other topics in astronomy or if these were simply newer stories that had as yet escaped the deadening dullness of textbook instruction. The science books adopted in most schools transmit a body of knowledge with little attention to the bodies for whom that knowledge is intended. The very nature of such texts is unscientific. Static, linear, and nonparticipatory, they stand in stark contrast to the dynamic, cyclic, and directly involving mode of science that is so inviting to young children. These texts offer children no stories, no connections between forms and forces, between observers and observed. Without this profound connectivity which is the lifeblood of science, the body of scientific knowledge can be reduced to a corpse. Through a storytelling mode, scientific knowledge can be kept alive for children. The challenge, however, is to find enough storytellers.

References

Feynman, Richard P. "What is Science?" *The Physics Teacher*, 7 (1968): 313–20.
Romanyshyn, Robert D. "Psychotherapy as a Creative Process," *The Psychotherapy Patient*, in press.
Weiss, Malcolm. *Gods, Stars and Computers: Fact and Fancy in Myth and Science.* Garden City: Doubleday and Company, 1980.

[Language Arts *65, no. 3 (1988): 255–59*]

9 Storytelling

Children's Narrative Thought, at Home and at School

Richard Van Dongen

Narrative story is an important way that human beings use to build and shape their experiences; narrative is one mode of thinking. It is widely accessible to the very young as well as to the adult, in both oral contexts as well as literate, the everyday world as well as specialized areas of study, the informal pace of ongoing daily life as well as the formalized structures of institutions like schools, and the personal or social experience as well as the art form of literature. This widely based thought and language phenomenon is one important framework for understanding literacy and literary development in children. There are relationships which can guide planning in bringing children, literacy, and literature together.

A seventh grader writes a trickster tale:

Coyote and Little Bear

Long ago there was Little Bear who lived east of Acoma. He and Coyote were the best of friends. But Coyote always played tricks on Little Bear, but not one of the tricks was as mean as the one he now planned.

First, Coyote needed to gather large, round stones. Then he was to paint them red and make the stones apples. Next, he got other stones and painted them orange to look like big, juicy oranges. When Coyote saw his friend walk by, he offered Little Bear the delicious looking fruit and told him graciously to help himself to the fruit. Little Bear chose an apple and found it to be very heavy. The weight of the apple made Little Bear suspicious so he scratched his finger against the apple and found the paint to come off. When Coyote was not looking, Little Bear got an apple tucked in his pocket and bit into it. Coyote couldn't believe what he saw. Little Bear thanked Coyote for the delicious apple and went on his way. As soon as Little Bear was out of sight, Coyote took an apple and bit into it. He found it to be very hard. Coyote took another bite and started to howl and growl because he found his teeth had fallen out.

This is the reason why he is sad: He no longer has teeth and he lost a good friend (Boynton, Jensen, and Van Dongen 1985).

This written narrative is one from a collection created by seventh graders at Sky City School, Acoma Pueblo, during a study of trickster tales. The students and their teacher are all members of the same American Indian Pueblo cultural community. They shared orally many stories from within their own cultural context; in addition another teacher from outside of their culture visited frequently and read aloud a variety of trickster tales from around the world. When the students began writing their own tales, they freely borrowed from both of these influences. They used elements of the rich storytelling tradition in their own community. They also used influences from the literary narratives which they read, heard, and shared in their school setting through stories found in children's literature and textbooks. Literacy and literary development are inseparable dimensions for these students. They are using the narrative mode of thought to develop imagination based upon their constructed knowledge of the community's narratives and also those narratives used and valued in the school. They are competently using written language (literacy) in order to create imaginative, artfully shaped thought in story (literature).

In classrooms where there are many opportunities to engage in the narrative mode of thought, literacy and literature become an entity. For children encounter and use narratives in a variety of ways: (1) they tell and retell personal experiences, (2) they create stories in play and social experiences, (3) they read and listen to stories through literature, reading, and writing, and (4) they use and encounter narrative in texts where the narrative is used to explain an event, an idea, or some phenomenon.

The potential of literacy/literary experiences is enriched when students use narrative for thinking but draw from the narrative reservoirs of the community and school. The seventh grader telling the coyote and bear story is using these reservoirs. She is thinking and writing in the narrative mode, but at the same time she works with meaningful influences on her story which come from her culture (storytelling, Acoma geography, and Acoma stories about coyote) and her school (literate language found in traditional literary tales and literate language used in reading and writing).

Through exploration of the narrative mode of thought and the use of such thought in children's communities and schools, relationships between literacy and literary development become explicit. Both the enjoyment of literature and competence in literacy require children to: (1) use the narrative mode of thought (not exclusively, however) to build experience and knowledge about the world, (2) understand that the forms and uses of narratives within their cultural communities are those which storytellers and writers use to create literature as an art form, and (3) bring their narrative competence through reading and writing to bear upon the literary narrative, a form highly valued in schooling.

The Narrative Mode of Thought

Strategies required for literacy and literary competence are mirrored in discussions of both the personal, everyday experience narrative and the literary narrative. Narrative thought, a primary act of mind (Hardy 1978), involves active building of experience, and users bring their past wealth of experience to create the ongoing narrative. Narrative thought organizes experiences and content around human intention (Bruner 1985). Such organization requires patterns which are predictable and recognizable so that the users of narrative plan, anticipate, predict, and confirm. These strategies are required both in literacy competence and also in the aesthetic stance (Rosenblatt 1982) demanded of the reader of literature.

Through telling stories, humans build their experience of living. The representation of events in narrative discourse allows experience to become internalized and owned. Church (1961, p. 113) describes an event:

> The morning after the big dance, the telephone system is taxed while the matrons and adolescents exchange impressions until the event has been given verbal shape and so can enter into the corpus of their experience.

Not only is the past retold as story to give form and meaning to life, but so is the present. Also the future can be rehearsed or projected through such telling.

The narrative is an efficient way to organize experience and to respond to an event. An eight-year-old tells a personal experience story:

> After school at one, at two, at three-thirty, my mom never came, and I was just waiting outside and everybody left. And I went and called and nobody was there so I just waited, and later I called and my mom was there and she forgot I was at school (Westby, Maggart, and Van Dongen 1984).

She is personalizing experience, but even more is happening. She is moving toward a literary quality as she develops a feeling tone implicitly built through her story as she stretches the time: "at one, at two, at three-thirty." The listener, reader, and teller all bring more of their experience to the narrative than the literal, explicit meaning offered. The fleshing out of the character's emotions, the setting, and the tone of the story build through stretching the time pattern. A sparse narrative can trigger a great deal of meaning.

A gifted literary writer, V.S. Naipaul (1984, pp. 22, 23) explores this triggering of experience in an autobiographical narrative about his writing:

> . . . —I sat at the typewriter in the freelancers' room in the Langham Hotel, to try once more to be a writer. And luck was with me that afternoon. *Every morning when he got up Hat would sit on the banister of his back verandah and shout across 'What happening there, Bogart?'* Luck was with me, because that first sentence was so direct, so uncluttered, so without complications, that it provoked the sentence that was to follow. *Bogart would turn in his bed and mumble softly so that no one heard 'What happening there, Hat?'*

Naipaul explains:

> The first sentence was true. The second was invention. But together—to me, the writer—they had done something extraordinary. Though they had left out everything—the setting, the historical time, the racial and social complexities of the people concerned they had suggested it all, they had created the world of the street. And together, as sentences, words, they had set up a rhythm, a speed which dictated all that was to follow.

The efficiency of the two sentences creates a world partly from Naipaul's life experience growing up in Trinidad and partly from his imagination, and evokes this world in readers who construct the experience by fleshing out the sparse, uncluttered narrative with their own experience and knowledge of the world and their control of narrative form and use of language.

From these different perspectives of narrative study a continuum emerges. At one end are the very personal narratives of a more oral nature of discourse and at the other end are literary narratives of a more literate art form. Hardy (1978) suggests that the narrative acts of everyday are transferred by the storyteller and the writer to art from life. The mental activity required of the storyteller and writer to artfully, imaginatively shape a story is based in the personal stories people create and use to build their experiences of daily living. As children move into the literate forms of language and story, the thinking processes required for literacy and literature come with them from their oral narratives of personal experience. Meek (1982) says that storying is a central feature of the culture of childhood, and it has the formal characteristics of literature.

The human intentions at the core of narrative are played out through the patterns of narrative structure. Literary and linguistic studies describe narrative structures and relationships. Some of these structures are important for children's literacy and literary under-standings. There is a teller and tale (Scholes and Kellogg 1966), and the teller's presence is felt whether in the role as narrator or in the role as a participant. There are events (plot) and existents (characters and settings) (Chatman 1978). There are themes.

These elements are shaped and organized in narrative discourse. Applebee (1978) shows such organization around two aspects, chain-ing and centering, which give coherence to stories. Chaining shows relationships of events through time and causality. Centering shows how these events are linked to a special aspect such as a character or theme. Applications of adaptations of story grammar analyses (Peter-son and McCabe 1983) show a logical unfolding of story through such patterns as: initiating event, motive, attempt, and consequence.

Narrative thought requires understanding of the planning and goal behavior required in order that characters' intentions unfold through the patterns of narrative structure. A storyteller may build to a high point through orientation clauses, complicating actions, and evalua-tive clauses, and then eventually dwell on a highpoint followed by a resolution (Peterson and McCabe 1983). The storyteller may pause in temporal order, suspend action, and dwell upon the tension before a resolution. When children internalize and enjoy the play with such structures in the stories they read and hear, they can also begin to play with these structures in their own narrative productions.

Children who are becoming literate through narrative competence are also moving towards an aesthetic stance in their reading and writing. The rhythm and repetition of sound in literate language, the combinations of words to create a provocative image or emotion, and fresh visions created in the narrative form all lead children to an aesthetic experience of language, image, feeling, and idea. Rosenblatt (1982) describes this stance as part of the reading, writing, and literary experience which occurs during the experience as opposed to what might be gleaned in thought after the reading or writing is completed.

The use of the narrative mode of thought as a way to build experience and knowledge about the world is accessible to children as they move from personal oral experiences to the literary narrative. Narrative understanding, competence, and enjoyment not only sup-port the scope of children's literacy development but also the richness of their literary development.

Narrative in the Cultural Community

In addition to the personal experiences of daily living, children experience the cultural community through story. These stories range from the sacred to secular entertainment. They all hold a society's values and the way children will approach narrative which may or may not be closely matched with the literary texts of school.

Stories and storytelling are universal. Harvey Cox (1973), a theologian, states that humans have an innate need to have a story to live by. There are collective stories about a cultural group dealing with such questions as "who are we?" or "where did we come from?" There are the individual, personal stories which are testimony and deal with such a question as "what happened to me?"

The uses and forms of narratives differ significantly across cultures. Stories may be integral to the cultural fabric or serve merely as entertainment. The roles which narratives take within a culture can be viewed through: (1) uses in daily life, rituals, and traditions, (2) teachings and values about the "good life," and (3) entertainment. These cultural emphases influence how children take on narrative thought, how they approach the use of narrative in the school, and how they meet expectations of the school as to what is a good narrative in their reading and writing.

Striking differences in use and form of narratives across three cultures can be found by comparing three collections of Southwestern United States stories all collected and retold by Joe Hayes, a Southwest storyteller. Anglo-American ranching families, northern New Mexican Hispanic villagers, and native American Pueblo and Navajo tribes come to stories in different ways.

Anglo ranching families may tell stories as entertainment during family gatherings. These are often about the teller who pokes fun at himself or herself, or they are about people and events known to the group. These tales are often full of exaggerations; they are in the tall-tale tradition (Hayes 1986). Hispanic American stories may carry many beliefs and teachings about the culture, perhaps even be told at more special times with preparation of food and a piñon fire in the fireplace on a winter's night. Religious motifs and beliefs are central to the stories, and there are princes and princesses who came along with the stories to New Mexico, perhaps from Spain, hundreds of years ago (Hayes 1982).

Native American stories carry on traditions and rituals tightly woven into a cultural fabric and belief system. They often carry teaching and instruction about the cultural life. Sometimes the stories are part of special rituals to be told by certain people at certain times of the year. The introduction to a collection of coyote stories collected and compiled by the Navajo Curriculum Center, Rough Rock Demonstration School (Roessel and Platero 1968, pp. 7, 8) reminds readers:

> Coyote stories are connected with various ceremonies and are retold when those ceremonies are performed. . . . Because they are told only during the winter (defined as the period between the first frost in the fall and the first thunder in the spring), those who contributed the stories have requested that they be used only during the winter months for instructional purposes.

This is further corroborated in Barre Toelken's foreword to Brady's (1984) study of Navajo children's narratives:

> Even the hilarious coyote tales, which are told for entertainment and moral instruction, are thought of as potentially dangerous in the wrong hands: their wording is so powerful that they are used in healing rituals, and thus a witch can also misuse his or her power to injure and kill. (p. x)

Brady collected and analyzed stories told by Navajo children at school. She contends that the children reveal much of the value and belief system held throughout Navajo culture even though these stories were narrated in the foreign language of English and in the apparently alien atmosphere of school.

Other studies of children's narratives also show cultural shaping. Narrative form and use differ across the cultural groups of Heath's (1983) descriptions of a southern United States textile mill town. Trackton (black textile workers), Roadville (white Appalachian textile workers), and the townspeople (the managers, business people, and professional groups) as cultural groups used narratives differently from each other. Trackton and Roadville people told stories, but they structured them differently and judged them in different ways. Trackton stories are highly creative, fictionalized accounts; Roadville's are factual with little exaggeration. Trackton's assert individual strength and power; Roadville's reaffirm group membership and behavioral norms. By contrast the townspeople's children showed a strong literate tradition with story through reading aloud experiences, story hours, and imaginative play.

Scollon and Scollon (1984) have studied Athabaskan narratives and dispute those views that suggest these stories are of poor quality. The storyteller produces an "abstract" which then is fleshed out through mutual sense making among the participants. Without this insight which the Scollons call an "unfocused situation," the outside, naive listener sees or hears little which makes sense as story. By contrast, Cook-Gumperz and Green (1984) are able to show how the popular books created by Richard Scarry may influence many American children's narrative production. The books have segments or stanzas with additional vignettes or substories in the illustrations. Children were influenced in structuring their own stories by characteristics of the narratives in these books.

The use of narrative thought in a cultural community shapes children's narrative competence. For many children the reading aloud of storybooks has been an important influence; this engagement with literate narratives matches the expectations of schooling. For many children there are other uses and forms of narrative. Those cultural influences which involve basic beliefs and values shared through stories may profoundly shape how children approach the literary narrative in school. Such cultural influences need to be valued and appreciated by the school; for these influences can support literacy and literary development.

Narrative in the Classroom

Children's understandings and uses of narrative thought support their movement into literacy and literary competence. Teachers who are knowledgeable about this thought process and the strategies of mental activity which it requires recognize relationships to the strategies necessary for reading and writing and aesthetic engagement with literature. They can plan for the opportunities needed so that children over time can move from the personal experience narrative to the literary text.

Also, children come to school with narrative experience both in forms and uses. Some children's experiences are more oral and personal; others may be more literate and artfully shaped by literature. Knowledge of how children's cultural communities use and create stories is therefore necessary. With this knowledge, teachers bring sensitivity and understanding as to how to move children's narrative experiences in school to the more literary narrative.

Engagement with narrative thought is supported not only by literature-based reading and writing programs (Zaharias 1986), but also by a range of classroom contexts where narratives are created, shared, and valued. Such contexts include: (1) play, (2) telling and listening to stories, (3) reading and reading aloud, and (4) writing. Opportunities and settings in classrooms for engagement in social play and informal drama support children's use of story to develop their imaginations and narrative competence. Also, children's stories need to be shared with others who are genuinely interested and attentive. Both the telling and retelling of personal and cultural stories need to have a place in school so that they are perceived by children as valuable resources to use in reading and writing. Frequent experiences in both reading stories and listening to stories read aloud encourage children to internalize the forms and uses of narrative so that children come to literature for enjoyment. With so many experiences with narrative thought children then have a resource for shaping and organizing their thoughts and imaginations through their writing.

Understandings of the narrative mode of thought and uses of narratives in cultural communities and in classrooms help children and teachers together move from the more oral to the more literate and from the more personal to the more literary art form of literature. Reading and writing competence (literacy) is part of this movement to more literary understandings and appreciations of literature.

References

Applebee, Arthur. *The Child's Concept of Story.* Chicago: The University of Chicago Press, 1978.

Boynton, Donna, Charlotte Jensen, and Richard Van Dongen. "Trickster Tales across the Language Arts Curriculum." Paper presented at the annual meeting of the New Mexico Council of the International Reading Association, Hobbs, NM, 1985.

Brady, Margaret K. *"Some Kind of Power": Navajo Children's Skinwalker Narratives.* Salt Lake City, UT: University of Utah Press, 1984.

Bruner, Jerome. "Narrative and Paradigmatic Modes of Thought." In *Learning and Teaching the Ways of Knowing,* edited by Elliot Eisner. Chicago: The University of Chicago Press, 1985.

Church, Joseph. *Language and the Discovery of Reality.* New York: Random House, 1961.

Cook-Gumperz, Jenny, and Judith L. Green. "A Sense of Story: Influence on Children's Storytelling Ability." In *Coherence in Spoken and Written Discourse,* edited by Deborah Tannen. Norwood, NJ: Ablex, 1984.

Cox, Harvey. *The Seduction of the Spirit.* New York: Simon and Schuster, 1973.

Hardy, Barbara. "Towards a Poetics of Fiction: An Approach through Narrative." In *The Cool Web,* edited by Margaret Meek, Aidan Warlow, and Griselda Barton. New York: Atheneum, 1978.

Hayes, Joe. *The Checker Playing Hound Dog.* Santa Fe, NM: Mariposa Publishing, 1986.

——. *The Day It Snowed Tortillas.* Santa Fe, NM: Mariposa Publishing, 1982.

Heath, Shirley Brice. *Ways with Words.* Cambridge, UK: Cambridge University Press, 1983.

Meek, Margaret. "What Counts as Evidence in Theories of Children's Literature?" *Theory into Practice,* 21 (1982): 284–92.

Naipaul, V. S. *Finding the Centre.* London: Andre Deutsch, 1984.

Peterson, Carole, and Allyssa McCabe. *Developmental Psycholinguistics: Three Ways of Looking at a Child's Narrative.* New York: Plenum Press, 1983.

Roessel, Robert A., and Dillon Platero (Editors). *Coyote Stories of the Navajo People.* Chinle, AZ: Dine, 1968.

Rosenblatt, Louise. "The Literary Transaction: Evocation and Response." *Theory into Practice,* 21 (1982): 268–77.

Scholes, Robert, and Robert Kellogg. *The Nature of Narrative.* New York: Oxford University Press, 1966.

Scollon, Ron, and Suzanne B.K. Scollon. "Cooking It Up and Boiling It Down: Abstracts in Athabaskan Children's Story Retellings." In *Coherence in Spoken and Written Discourse,* edited by Deborah Tannen. Norwood, NJ: Ablex, 1984.

Westby, Carol, Zelda Maggart, and Richard Van Dongen. "Language Prerequisites for Literacy Development." Paper presented at the meeting of The Third International Congress for the Study of Child Language, Austin, TX, 1984.

Zaharias, Jane Ann. "Implications of a State-wide Survey of Children's Literature Instruction." *The CLA Bulletin,* 12 (1986): 10–13.

[Language Arts *64, no. 1 (1987): 79–87*]